FACTORS INFLUENCE TOURISM DEVELOPMENT

JOHN LOK

Made with ❤ on the Notion Press Platform
www.notionpress.com

Contents

Preface

Introduction

Nowadays, global tourism industry is experiencing decline stage or decline life cycle stage due to COVID19 human hung disease occurs. It brings many travelers begin to feel fear to catch air planes because any one passenger may be gotten this kind of new disease when one or more than one passenger who had owned this kind of new lung disease and he/she is or they are sitting in the air plane. So, many travelers believed that when one owned COVID 19 lung disease passenger is catching in any one air plane, it will have high chance that they will be contacted to give this kind of disease easily by the air in the closed windows airplane. Due to this reason, this kind of new disease had influenced global many travelers felt fear to catch air planes to go to different countries to travel in these two years, even future. However, whether COVID 19 disease is the main factor to influence global tourism industry decline and oil price changes. It is one interesting question to research.

Hence, this kind of new disease can bring these questions to global tourism industry development and fuel need, such as: Can travelers number influence fuel price whether it raises up or falls down? If it was sure that tourism industry recession or growth up, it can have direct or indirect relationship to cause fuel price increasing or decreasing effect, whether what are the main factors to cause tourism industry development or recession can influence fuel price rises up or falls down? Why and how traveler traveling leisure behavior can influence fuel price increases or decreases or fuel need increases or decreases to airline industry?

In my this book, I shall attempt to apply behavioral economic theory to explain why and how traveler individual catching air planes leisure activities or travelling leisure need or leisure activities, they have direct or indirect relationship to influence future fuel price changes. Readers can attempt to follow behavioral economic view to explain whether traveler individual leisure activities can have any relationship to influence future global fuel need changes or price changes.

Prologue

Table of contents

CHAPTER ONE

Terrorism attack and fuel price raising influences tourism industry development

Nowaday, airline industry is entering global competition. So, any some less positive or negative social environment changing which will influence any airlines' passenger behavioral consumption change. For example, air ticket price rises or fuel price rises or the country's season is bad or the global economy is bad or the country has terrible death threat etc. different negative social environment change fastors which will influence any country passenger individual travel consumption desires.

In Special, business class airline transportation demands are also increasing, due to many business travelers need to catch planes to go to any different countries to do business as well as many cargoes need to be carried from planes to transport to different countries to sell. So, business class traveler target group behavioral consumption is difficult to influence travelling consumotion desires from external environmental factors because business class traveler target group concerns to need to catch planes to go to another country to discuss business co-operation with the country's businessmen. So, their business travel desires won't easy to be influenced more than individual entertainment travel consumer's desire.

It seems cargo and business aim of aviation transportation industry has less chance to be influenced to reduce businessmen traveler or cargo transportation numbers to compare to entertainment traveler numbers by external environment change influences, due to the business travelers and cargo transportation travelling desires is difficult to reduce travelling or transportation needs to reduce the " doing businesses to earn profit chance with another country's businessmen". However, ignorance of internal or external market dynamics, catching entertainment travelers business can be detrimental to airline profitability more than carrying cargoes or business travelers business. Because the demands of travelling different countries' travelers' consumption are still more than the demands of businessmen carrying cargoes in any countries every year. So, the global GDP of travelling income sector is still have the important position to any country nowadays.

How can positive or negative social environment change influence any airlines' air ticket prices to be risen or fallen as well as how can these social environment change influence passenger consumption desires ? For example: What is the petroleum price change influence ?In fact, the increase in petroleum price can have chance to affect every airlines passenger has a negative manner to reduce travel consumption because increased oil prices have resulted in the reduction of airline services operations, the number of airline schedules flights, even airline bankruptcies. Whether global economic inflation or deflation, terrorism threats to the country, oil shortage or oil price rising or fallening, bank interest rate increasing or decreasing etc. external factors which have the most influential causes to bring the bad or good effects to cause airline industry share price reducing or increasing or increasing or reducing air ticket price. In result, these external environmental changes will influence the global traveler numbers to be increased or decreased at the time.

To support this hypotheses, this are my research first question, such as : Does a combination of terrorism and price of petroleum significantly influence airline profit changing mostly? The alternative hypothesis was my research second question, such as: Whether a significant relationship exists between terrorism, price of petroleum and airline profitability more than other factors, such as inflation, bank interest rate or air ticket price changing of these factors to influence passenger consumption desires change. I shall indicate that the first assumption was that terrorism has a negative effect on airline profitability and another assumption was that only external factors as oil prices or terrorism affect airline profitability. Finally, the terrorism and oil shortage and oil rising price factors can influence every passenger travel consumption desire to be reduced mainly.

Terrorism attack influences traveller need

However the effects of oil price and terrorism on airline profitability was limited to a regional perspective, so oil price and terrorism external environmental change will only influence some countries' airline traveler numbers to be decreased, e.g. the terrorism attack of plane crash event to USA on 11 Sept. After the terrorism attack happened on USA 11 Sept. incident of terrorism attack was restricted to events of skyjacking, attacks on oil production, refinery and distribution. Then, due oil shortage will be caused due to reducing oil production, refinery and distribution as well as it will influence oil price is risen and airline ticket price is also risen. It will reduce travel consumption desire to some countries if their airlines' ticket prices are also increasing. Other types of terrorist activities, such as attacks on financial targets or senior government officials could have an adverse effect on the petroleum and airline industry. I think the disruption of the production or distribution of petroleum because of incidents of terrorism was costly in terms of loss of business and the inflationary effect on fuel dependent products or services.

In fact, some airlines have adopted more fuel saving technology, so whose fuel consumption would not use more than other non fuel saving technology airlines. It seems fuel price increasing will not be the only factor to influence the airline industry's traveler numbers decreasing due, the owning more fuel saving technologic airlines which air tickets prices won't influence to be risen , due to reducing oil production and shortage influences . However, due to some airlines which have fuel saving technology, so which can avoid to use more fuel to provide planes to use and which fuel costs will be reduced, then which can provide cheaper air ticket fare prices to compare the non fuel saving technology airlines. The result will cause some not owning fuel saving technological airlines which will lose travelling customers in this global airline travelling market, also the not fuel saving technological airlines need to renew their fuel technology if which want to keep their competitive abilities to avoid to close down their businesses. So, what factors will influence the not owning fuel saving technological airlines profitability to be reduce if the oil shortage factor can not influence their planes energy supply to be reduced to cause air ticket prices to be increased? To answer this question, I shall indicate another financial risk factor how it influences airline industry behavioral change.

Also, I shall indicate the financial risk of airline industry evidence from Cathay Pacific airways and China airlines against key determinants of which include interest rate, exchange rate and fuel price risk for the period of January 1996 year to December 2011 year. During this period, these key external factors which were the most serious influence to cause these two airlines choose to change their strategic behaviors. Due to any these financial risks is difficult to predict and it was also changing often, these factors will also affect any airlines stock returns which arise from changing economic conditions, e.g. fuel price movements and fluctuations in exchange rates. These external unpredicted changing factors will attribute to the air tickets cyclical demand, capital investment, fixed costs of labor and landing rights to this global airline industry. Finally, it will cause some airlines need to rise air ticket prices to reduce expenditures increasing.

However, the relationship between fuel price and stock prices varies across economies which will influence travel passenger consumption of desires. For example, the effects of oil price changes in sub-sector indices, such as wood, paper and printing, insurance and electricity. In the past, on global stock exchange market was positively significant in 2011 year. Otherwise, with respect to the U.S.A. aviation industry, some economists suggested that global airlines stock returns were negatively to percentage change in fuel prices related to any airline firm value, e.g. Qantas and Air New Zealand were negatively share price growth to fuel price risk in the short term in the 2011 year. Thus, due to these two airlines share price went down, it will influence investors who loss confidence to buy their shares as well as it will influence travelling passengers who choose to buy other airlines' air tickets to go to travel because they will feel these two airlines have business challenges, e.g. bad service quality and food quality and uncomfortable airline seat environment and poor management style. etc different bad feeling. So, these two airlines' share prices went down, it will influence every travel passenger's confidence to choose to buy their air tickets to sit their planes to go to travel.

Airlines fuel manufacturing supply strategy

However, there are some airlines which are the characteristic of self organization . It means that they are present in that both of oil fuel production and providing flights service in airline industry. So, these self organization airlines can control the oil fuel price by themselves. However, any self supply airline organization is also evident in efforts by businesses acts of terrorism against economic targets by adopting proactive steps, such as airline and airport security. So, it seems any self suply airline organization can reduce the risk to avoid oil price raising and terrorism attacks in airline industry risk management sector because oil shortage won't influence their air ticket prices need to be raised. Beside, these self supply airline organizations which have high technology of fuel efficient aircrafts, the use of one aircraft model, the adoption of direct routes versus customer loyalty programs and other operational cost reductions are strategies for increased profitability.

To solve oil price, terrorism etc. external risk to airline industry. Instead of high technology of fuel efficient aircrafts and self supply airline organization methods can solve terrorism attacks and oil price rising risks. However, I believe that there are other risks will threaten to airline industry. This risks concern traveller individual psychological factors influence, so it means that any airlines can apply psychological methods to predict which airline passengers' travel consumption desires. The risks include such as (1) user factor, such as : the travel country culture and tradition difference will influence the traveler chooses to prefer to go to the country to travel , the traveler's education level is high , who will choose to go to developed countries to travel, e.g. USA, UK. Otherwise, if the traveler's education level is low, who will choose to go to developing countries to travel, e.g. China, India etc. (2) economic factor, such as air tickets and airline fuel costs, (3) human resources and macro economic factor, such as political stability, economic development, educational policy, health policy, environmental policy. However, these risks occurrences are resulting in the relationship of cause and effect events. These events are not directly observable.

Such as, the complexity of relationship between terrorism and airline profitability. Hence, if global airline industry can predict when those risks occur to do protective strategic behavior. It is possible that which can understand why these risk events will occur and their protective strategic behaviors also influence their outcomes to be positive to avoid any external risk threats on the long term. However, I think hierarchy, self supply airline organization efficiency methods which are as possible predictors of user preferences to avoid risk threat events to cause whose airline businesses failure occurrences in airline industry because it can reduce oil shortage factor which causes their air ticket prices need to be rised to keep their planes can have enough fuel supply.

● Why tourism and airline industries have close relationship to influence their profitability between of them.

In my study, I suppose terrorism, profitability and the price of petroleum which had properties of distinct and interrelated close relationship. Moreover, these variables (terrorism, profitability and the price of petroleum) displayed differentiation, self replication, efficiency and hierarchy which can cause risk events to airline industry. However, I also think the other internal and external threat factors of airline industry, such as inflation, bank interest rate, business model, service quality, airline fuel or plane engine technology, air ticket pricing, brand loyalty, airline strategic management, government policy and fuel hedging of these factors which can also raise the risks to threaten any airlines existence in airline industry.

There are two basic business models in airline industry. They are network (full service) and low cost (discount) carriers. The network carrier model employs diversification strategy by increased domestic destinations, serving international routes, providing diverse seating arrangements (business, economy and first class), maintaining a complex system of offering high quality service. Otherwise, low cost (discount) airlines focus on lower air fares. To keep operating costs down, discount airlines offer shorter routes and provide point-to-point destinations rather than through sophisticated flights are primarily in domestic destinations. So, discount airlines operate a common model aircraft fleet, offer a single seating arrangement and cheaper flight services offered to compare network airlines. However, these two basic business models have their unique competitive abilities to provide any airlines existence in airline industry nowadays.

In fact, natural resource of oil is decreasing in our earth. But as the same time, human demand is increasing and oil supply is decreasing, so it also causes the oil fuel price is increasing to supply to airline industry. It influences not only to airline industry, it also impacts of higher oil fuel price to tourism, such as expansion of airports are made based on expected demand increase.

Tourism has been proven to many adverse events, including terrorism, flight disruptions. Beside, the bad natural climate change influences, such as the volcanic ash cloud event occurred in April 2010 year. So, airline industry need to concern climate change because it will cause high fuel prices indirectly. For example, the event occurred the extreme increase in operating costs for airlines in 2008 year, due to unprecedented prices for aviation fuel also meant, that despite the introduction of fuel charges, so this event causes the global airline industry recorded losses seriously. Even if alternative fuels become commercially available for airlines which are still likely to be more expensive than present aviation fuel. Thus, it seems that poor tourism will influence poor travel consumption and low airline tickets sale.

Higher airfares in the future are likely to lead to reduction in travel and cause tourists to shift from more distant to closer destination. When some of the economic responses to higher oil prices are obvious assessing the overall economic impacts on tourism is difficult. However, long term changes in global oil price rises will be similar to global changes in other commodity prices, exchange rates and income. It is therefore important to consider the impact of high oil prices on tourism from a general equilibrium perspective rather than relying only on bottom partial equilibrium. However, I believe tourism and airline industries have close relationship, such as tourism and airline industries are likely to suffer in an environment of high oil prices. Given that tourism destinations receive tourists from a range of origins, it would be useful to understand of some countries are increasing oil prices than others. Such as the net oil importing countries are selling higher oil prices than oil exporting countries generally. For example, New Zealand is an oil import country to provide planes for international visitor arrivals, so its oil fuel price is usually higher to charge to NZ airlines because any NZ airlines need to pay to foreign countries to buy any oil more expensive price. So, NZ airlines usually charge higher airfares to its visitors to compare the other exporting oil countries' airlines.

In economic theory, on income effects indicate negative impacts on tourism demand, the exact effects of higher oil fuel prices for specific destinations are far from clear. However, airline industry's different market segments show different sensitivities to air ticket fares changes. On the first hand, if the visitors are long destinations generally wealthier than average and therefore potentially less affected, as energy costs would be a smaller proportion of their income compared will be those from less wealthy groups. On the second hand, oil prices don't translate into higher transport costs especially not on air routes that are highly competitive and that are maintained for strategic reasons. On the third hand, many other factors shape tourists' decision making, including emotion drivers or those related to images, fashions and perceptions.

Increasing environmental protection awareness of tourists could also be an important factor to influence tourism consumption, instead of oil fuel price raising causes air ticket fares raising factor to reduce traveler numbers. However, oil price raising reason causes also due to high use of cars, vans and domestic air transport in some countries, e.g. Hong Kong, China countries, there are many people like to buy cars to drive. So, the private driver numbers are increasing demand to cause these countries' oil fuel prices raise in the short time suddenly. It will influence HK and China air tickets prices need to be risen , due to there are many cars, vans and domestic air transport tools need to use oil to supply energy to cause oil import numbers will increase to HK and China and HK and China airlines need to pay higher price to buy oil to use. In the result, HK and China airlines air ticket prices will also need to rise and it will influence HK and China travel consumption desire.

Fuel raising price solve methods

● Why oil fuel raising price factor can cause risk to airline.

In long run, implications of changes to supply and demand side conditions of oil fuel energy may differ qualitatively. For example, due to investment responses of producers, consumers and governments in alternative energy sources and more energy efficient plants, vehicles are supplied in order to achieve oil fuel price can't be risen seriously.

However, I believe oil fuel rising charge will be an important factor to influence global airline ticket fares to be also increased. Firstly, on the bank interest changing factor, e.g. bank interest rate rising which only attract more bank saving. But it can not influence the bank savers who choose to reduce relax time to go to other countries travelling. Otherwise, when the bank savers can save more money to earn higher interest in banks, who will prefer to choose to use their saving to consume travelling. Due to who can earn higher interest rate after a period of saving time. So, I believe whose behavioral travelling consumption will be raised when the banks will raise interest rate, then the bank savers won't choose to save more money in banks. So it is possible that who will withdraw more money to consume to go to travelling from their bank saving. It seems bank interest rate changing won't influence bank savers' behavioral travelling consumption to be reduced. Secondly, on the exchange rate changing factor, although any country's exchange changing will cause other countries' money value to be fallen down or risen up. However, it won't influence any travelers' behavioral consumption to be reduced seriously. Although, it is possible that the traveler won't spend too much to go to shopping when who travel to the another country and arrive the country. But, it is not possible to influence the traveler decides to reduce consumption to buy any air ticket to go to travelling. Thirdly, any country inflation also can not reduce travelers' travelling consumption easily because inflation can influence consumers who choose to buy cheaper foods and clothing and reduce entertainments in their every day life. But, one country's inflation can not influence it's citizen do not spend much travelling expenditure because travelers only spend one time or two times of travelling every year usually. So, the travelling expenditure rate of any households is not too much to compare daily essential expenditure. So, it seems that bank interest rate and exchange rate changing and inflation factors won't influence any travelers' travelling consumption of decisions to be reduced easily. Otherwise, if the oil fuel price raises too much, then global airlines' cost will be raised. So, the airlines only choose to increase their air fare prices to aim to avoid loss possibly. It seems that oil fuel price has direct influence airline income.

● Methods to solve rising air fare prices demand.
    I. Why will biofuels energy be demanded ?
I suggest these methods how to avoid the oil raising price factor to cause airline air fare prices to be risen to lead the risk of traveler numbers to be reduced.

The first method: Whether aviation fuel markets will have what benefits from biofuels supply to planes. I shall refer the scope includes trends in jet fuel price, airline response to fuel price, increases and volatility and environmental goals for aviation. The aviation fuel supply industry includes production, distribution and consumption of aviation fuel and it outlines players in the aviation fuel supply chain. For example, at each airport, fuel supply chain organization and fuel sourcing could differ with regard to the role of oil companies, airlines, airport owners and operators and airport service companies. However, major jet fuel purchasers are airlines, general aviation operators, corporate aviation and the military, with most of the jet fuel in global different countries demanders being used for domestic commercial and civilian flights carrying passengers, cargos or both. Commercial aviation fuel efficiency has improved dramatically over time, largely due to aircraft and engine upgrades and operational and air traffic control improvements. So, it seems that fuel supply factor can influence airline fare prices majorly.

However, jet fuel prices generally correlate with prices of crude oil and other refined petroleum products, such as diesel. So, increasing prices and the persistent price volatility of jet fuel markets import airline industry finances in any countries. However, airlines use various strategies to manage aviation fuel price certainty, including financial hedges, increased vertical integration and adjustments in aircraft utilization and size to avoid the jet fuel raising price risk. Investments in alternative aviation fuel could be a mechanism to diversity expose to the price of petroleum. It seems the use of alternative aviation fuel would serve to diversify the fuel mix to reduce the risk of jet fuel monopoly raising price threat. If a diversified fuel mix were to avoid either fuel raising price in short term or to avoid fuel raising price in long term. Potential benefits include reduced actual fuel costs from only choice of jet fuel supply increased price certainty and lessened fuel costs. This diversify could allow airlines to become more consistently profitable and to make other investments in their businesses.

So, biofuels have potential to meet aviation industry needs, possibly including managing risks of upward fuel price trends and fuel price volatility and avoid risks with greenhouse gas emissions. So, the aviation fuels market could use biofuels to reduce greenhouse gas emission and mitigate long-term upward price trends, fuel price volatility or both.

What are the challenges of high priced oil for aviation? In fact, nowadays not the resources of oil as such, but much more the insecurity of supply, due to geopolitical instability in combination with a tight oil market makes a scenario with much higher oil prices than the world is currently experiencing not unlikely. Aviation is completely dependent upon oil as its fuel source. Since no practical energy substitute is readily available for commercial aviation, a scarcity of petroleum relative to demand will present a major aviation policy. In addition, efficiency gains, due to operational measures and new aircraft medium term. In particular, it has been demonstrated that the annual reduction rate in fuel consumption traffic unit is not a constant, but is itself also falling, in contrast to past estimates.

So, a high-priced oil scenario will have severe consequences for demand, airline revenues, the competitive position of airports and eventually airline networks, strategies and fleet development. In particular, transfer demand, short-haul and leisure traffic can be expected to be heavily affected by high oil prices, due to their relative high price sensitivity. So, different countries' governments or/and airlines are valuable to research another new and potential biofuel energy to substitute oil energy to supply our planes to reduce the threat of oil monopoly supply to influence the cause of air fare raising prices. Because the elasticity is very high to travelers, when the travelers feel air fares are rising high or even low level to influence travelers who will choose not to buy the air tickets to go to travel easily.

Will the fuel (oil based inputs) risk be higher to compare other costs to cause air ticket prices to be increased?, e.g. engineering maintenance, employees salaries, general cleaning, security office expenses etc. expenditures to airlines? If the probability-weighted upside effect on firm value when a risk is resolved favorably is greater the risk than the probability-weighted downside effect if the risk is resolved badly, then expected value work not be enhanced by hedging. So, the risk will be resolved badly to any commercial airlines. Airlines are an interesting case because the direct effect of source of risk resides squarely within the no offset in revenue functions (unlike for oil producers, for example), so value effects from costs feed directly into equity value. Most directly, the risk source is fuel costs to commercial airlines. Jet fuel is of course, a mix product of crude oil, so airlines indirectly face oil price risk. There are reasons to expect that airlines' fuel costs might to convex in oil price (i.e. absent any hedging). For example, oil prices, being generally pro-cyclical in recent times, tend to be highest when airline demand is strong. Airlines are therefore apt to use more high priced fuel than low-priced fuel over time. Airlines can raise air fare benefit is limited by the elasticity of demand. Also, cost functions could be influenced from fuel cost corresponds to upturns in economic activity overall (due to demand pressures on oil related prices), so it causes that airline's capacity delivers their services given their level of fixed capital. The essence of airlines basis risk in the case of jet fuel is essentially the time profile of the refining margin between crude and jet fuel, or the time profile of the price differential between other refined distillates and jet fuel. Thus, it is far from clear that risk management with oil is sure to add value to any airlines. It seems the impact of airline energy and any countries' domestic or foreign airline passenger travel numbers which have direct close relationship.

II. Whether the relationship between terrorism and oil prices has close relationship.

Whether the relationship between terrorism and oil prices has close relationship. It needs to judge to determine if a combination of terrorism and the price of petroleum significantly predicted airline profitability and which variable whether the further period was the most significant between the terrorism occurrence and the price of petroleum influence. So, different countries' governments or airlines need to collect samples of financial records from which country's any airline commercial passengers and cargo airlines on costs of fuel and any airline profitability. Also, gathering the terrorism data were comparison of terrorist attacks on petroleum in oil-producing nations, and incidents of high jacking aboard any country's aircraft. When any countries' airlines or governments can judge whether the impact of airline energy and terrorism risk level is high or middle or low level. Then, which can use this sample data to measure how to do positive social change to whether to increase or reduce employment in commercial aviation industry, or ought need to invest other higher commercial activity in tourist and other travel related service businesses and when is the most right time to adopt of green technologies by the civil aviation manufacturing industry after the terrorism attacks occurrence to any country. It seems that any countries' governments or airlines which ought concern that the event of when the terrorism attacks will occur and gather past sample data to predict when the next time terrorism attacks event will be occurred and the risk will be high or middle or low level to influence global airline industry development.

III. What factors will influence airline industry's price elasticity of supply and demand?

In fact, the airline industry is largely dependent on the supply of the oil industry. Otherwise, the oil industry is inelastic. However, the increase or decrease of the price of airfare is directly related to the increase or decrease of the oil's price to fuel the aircrafts because there has no any new energy which can be substituted to oil fuel to airline industry. So, it seems oil fuel producers are monopolies to control its sale price to be raised easily.

Another factor that can affect airline industry to be directly targeted by a tragedy brought about by terrorism. The past four years, from 2001 year to 2005 year, there had been at least $40 billion worth of losses in the airline industry because of the September 11 date terrorism attacks in 2000 year. There had been an expected and significant decrease in the demand for the airline industry services because of the attacks that involved planes hijacking and crashing into key locations like the World Trade Center and the Pentagon in USA. Although, terrorism attacks can bring risk to influence fuel price rising in airline industry. However, this risk occurrence to airline industry is only that after the terrorism attacks occurred. It is possible that terrorism attacks won't occur again in the future.

Otherwise, our concerning ought be the greenhouse emissions and how it affects global warming. The air quality would be better once this new regulations are adopted. However, it would affect large airlines. So, it would increase the price of airfares because of economic fees that airline companies have to cover. Air pollution can give a negative impact on the domestic or oversea owned airline companies for long term. If airlines' planes can use clean fuel to fly, e.g. biofuel, then it will bring benefits to global airlines for long term. On the positive side, the environment would be healthier as the earth's temperature would rise, and greenhouse effect would be dramatically reduced. This positive effect can come at a cost that is greater than most people perceive. So, the environment protection travellers who will reduce travelling times to avoid air pollution is caused to influence human health. It seems that airlines need to concern to apply psychological method to predict whose travelling consumption of behavior which is more suitable than behavioral economy method.

On the psychology view point on travelers, who will be more preferable to catch planes to go to different countries to travel, due to the chance of air pollution and global environmental warm issues will be reduced to low risk to influence our health if planes can use biofuel to be energy to fly in the future one day. It seems that spending expenditure to research other non polluted biofuel new energy is one solvable method to global airline industry in the future. To solve, any airlines or countries' governments or oil producers ought choose to spend more time to research new biofuel. Otherwise, the predicting when terrorism attacks event will be occurred, it is more difficult to predict the time more than researching to produce new biofuel energy method in the future.

So, I recommend that researching the new biofuel energy or other kinds of energy to substitute the oil energy and air pollution risk these two factors are the urgent behavioral economy method is used to solve this challenge which the airlines or oil producers or different countries' governments which need to concern nowadays. Because these two negative environment factors are the most influential to cause traveller individual travelling consumption desire to be fallen among of other negative environment factors.

CHAPTER TWO

Tourism service influences tourism industry development

The main cost related factors to offline or online travel agents

Nowadays,many online or offline travel agents have interest to find what the main factors that can affect their strategies to reduce airline costs. The main factors include route structure, type and characteristics of the aircracft, cost of labor and management quality, which will influence whether which airline routes are the most suitable to let online travel agents or offline travel agents to help them to sell paper air tickets or electronic air tickets to attract travel consumption more easily.

Thus, a cost-related strategy is the main important factors to influence travel consumption choice between online or offline travel agents. For example, considering that advantages in costs is an important strategy for carriers to remain in travel transportation market.

The deregulation process of travel markets and increasing opportunities for competition have created excess capacity in many markets that causes lower rates, even with its rising costs. Thus, the travel strategic costs management as well as travel consumers that their behavior under different influences can bring competitive advantages over travel players.

Cost reduction in the travel market -based industry is a very important way of being competitive between offline and online travel agents, when facing travel air ticket prices decreasing for every trip. So reduce to total travel cost, e.g. fuel, maintenance, labor etc. is relevant, but the influence of each component on every total trip cost depends on factors that are related or not to airline operation. For example, some airline can adopt the lowest cost model to sell air tickets from offline or online travel agents which compete for travel passengers with traditional modes as self driving road transport trip in large areas of countries domestic travel market, such as US, UK domestic travel market.

However, the decision about the relevance of one cost is not a simple matter. The effectiveness of reduction of each item that comprises the total cost of airline can change over time, depending on both the business model and the scope of the airline company or online /offline travel agent company as well as external factors.

However, there are three types of competition advantage between online and offline travel market: They are such as agility, differentiation cost and the differentiation may be related to a product of superior quality, higher value f the brand or the company's positive reputation. Such as the online travel agent's providing the different airline cheap air ticket price and kind of trips to provide to travel consumer consumer comparison or the offline travel agent's famous brand or positive reputation to let travel consumers feel travel agents can provide many actual trip package to let them to compare by oral clearly. Thus, the online travel agent's weakness is lack of travel agent individual exploration to let every travel consumer to understand every trip package more clearly.

But online travel agent's strength is it can provdide one website to let travel consumer attempt to compare different trip air ticket and/or hotel price to make personal travel pre-booking decision at home. The another advantage is related to techniques that reduce production cost, making it is possible to offer cheaper air ticket, or hotel room rents, or cheap trip package, than the competition.

Such as online travel agent can sell more cheap electronic air ticket price to compare traditional offline travel agent's paper air ticket price.

Finally, agility refers to the speed which the company responds to market demands. For example, if the online travel agent can make statistics to analyze how many online travel consumers to choose to buy which airlines' electronic or paper air tickets, e.g. which airline trip destinations and trips and hotels choices are the most popular attraction to them. Then, the online airline has possible to respond to provide to the most popular airline trips choices, electronic air ticket price comparison choices and hotel rooms prices choices to attract many online travel consumers to enter their online travel websites to choose different airline electronic tickets to buy or pre-book hotel rooms from travel agent websites. Also, if the traditional offline travel agents can attempt to gather every travel consumer's destination trips, hotels , airline paper or electronic ticket prices enquires to make statistics to make which travel trip journeys or destinations and airline paper travel ticket prices are the most popular. Then, it is possible that they can respond to every travel consumer individual demand more to attract whose travel agent choice more easily.

Airline travel agency AirAsia in the domestic airline low cost strategy

There are three major characteristics of the airline industry namely is product nature, its expenditure structure and its market entry conditions. Airline agent's product is homogeneous or undifferentiated , causing significant competition in airline domestic travel or foreign travel both markets, which are free from regulations and economic barriers. However, high capital and operating expenditure is another important characteristic of the airline industry. Aircrafts, airlines' major capital expenditure are very costly to acquire . For operating expenditures, aviation fuel and labor make up the two major costs in the industry.

Another important characteristic of the airline industry is the conditions for market entry, which differs between international and domestic airline markets . In the international travel market, airline travel agency entry is very difficult as international flights and routes are the results of regotiations between governments . On the other hand, in the domestic and regional travel market, travel agency entry depends on the level of deregulation or liberalisation. More and more countries, however are opening up their domestic travel markets for more competition. In addition, government plays an important role to regulate the travel markets and existing players may significant influence over now travel agent entrants.

In fact, the mjor factors influence to international or domestic travel consumption increasing numbers are the global economy and safety issues, instead of other different economic factors, such as travel destination choice, electronic air ticket or paper air ticket price, hotel price , the country's political change, e.g. war occurrence, bad weather , e.g. very cold or very hot etc. different factors infuence. Because generally , the world or any region of it is in an economic crisis or depression , the demand for airline services will fall. The late 1990 year Asian financial crisis for example, resulted in minimal increase in the number of worldwide airline passengers incrased only minimally from 1997 to 1998 year. Another factor of influencing the travel passenger number to be decreased, it concerns safety issues are also an important driver of the travel industry, which is subject to very safety standards to influence travel passengers' travel choice to the country. In addition, they are also unexpected safety related events, such as the 11 Sept. 2001 year tragedy in the US, which caused reduction in passengers . The increasing popularity of low cost airlines is the newest trend in the airline industry if which hope many passengers choose to buy whose electronic air ticket or paper air ticket to catch which planes to fly from online travel agent or offline travel agent channels.

The rise of low cost airlines, such as AmericaWest, JetBlue and Airtran in US, Ryanair and EasyJet in Europe and Vigin Blue in Australia. The share of low cost airline strategy is popular in the US and European airline market. For example, the Southwest airline low cost strategy is the basis of most low cost airlines operations. The key of the strategy is to reduce costs when at the same time offering low prices to passengers. History showed that the low cost airline strategy is easy to replicate , but difficult to implement successfully.

However, I suggest airlines need to know what functions which can attract passengers to chose to catch their planes to fly if they expect to rise passenger numbers. For example, the critical function of the Malaysia airline travel is to connect the major towns and remote interior areas within East Malaysia, which has poor road systems and limited availability of other significant means of transportation . In contrast, West Malaysia has more developed and extensive rod and railway systems.

Therefore, airline travel is not the main mode of long distance transportation. It implies Malaysis airline ought concentrate on focusing short distance transportation strategy for passenger beneficial choice function. For example, a new small Malaysia airline serving one or two routes may enter easily. Otherwise, a larger airline servicing multiple routes may be harder to enter Malaysia airline market. It also means access to capital and labor are the major obstacles for new airline entrants to Malaysia airline market. Thus, small airlines into a larger airline is probably more likely to be successful as in Air Asia's case to Malaysia airline market.

Thus, the airline low cost strategy competition positions include very low or minimal pressive from other airline similar service substitute products, low or medium power of airline similar input suppliers. In conclusion, low cost airline strategy is a god method to be attempted to win competitors in airline market.

How consumers select travel service between online and offline mode in travel industry

Nowadays, the travel industry is operating through two different modes, online and offline respectively. It involves the identification of the competitive strategies adopted by the tour operators. For example, it was found that e-retil travel is platform that is bringing two market forced the demand and supply tour operators and the customers together, and both parties and more inclined towards online mode in near future. Tour operators are gaining by operating at low cost and increasing their business reach when customers get what they desire as per their convenience. For example, many tour operators had promoted tourism destination through website that allow user to use interface for booking transporttion, foreign exchange etc. However, the role of travel operators (agents) should be assisted any airlines to promote their travel package service by internet more easily , such as tourism destination , arrangement of hospitality, restaurants, transportation tools during their trips.

The reasons why consumers choose online travel service include:

Firstly, it is online researching hospitality service. Online travel websites can provide many different accommodation furniture, such as seeking hotel locations, rooms prices comparison, prepaid hotel rooms by visa card payment transaction method, range from luxury five stars deluxe category hotels to small guest houses. The primary need of tourist is to find a place for residing in foreign country or domestic country to ensure whose safety and relaxing needs. Online travel website channel can help whom to find a place , according to his/her needs and paying capacity in the most shorten times.

Secondly, it is online restaurant (food and beverages researching) service. Full service restaurants are divided into two categories, fine dining and casual dining restaurants . Fine dining restaurants are usually located in the premises of luxury hotels, provide high quality food at premium price with good ambience and highly trained professionals. Thus, travel consumers can also compare the different restaurant food price and seek where is the restaurant and find.

What food taste of food supply from the travel agency or travel operator website easily 250 + tour operators are registered with the ministry of tourism (website of tourism ministry) , and the major players in the industry are dealing online and are dominating the travel industry. The major online travel players are Thomas cook,

Cox and Kings, make any trips, clear trip, gatra.com and Expedia. The tour operators whether online or offline offers a large number of services to the tourists including customized package where the customer selects each element of the tour package, specialized tourism package and complete tour guide package.

Nowadays, the tour operational travel (agents) are working through two different modes: offline online . Big brands with luge investment are dealing online and enjoying low cost benefits and huge profit margins. When the small tour operators have their market niche and managing have their market niche and managing their profits by dealing offline.

It is generally prefer offline mode that is the opportunity for small capital investment or employee number for tour operators. But the large scenario is changing as with the usage of internet by the tour operations have given convenience to the customers and now the customers of modern age have started developing preference for online modern. Thus, internet technology change any countries' travel agents or tour operators' air ticket sale method. So, it brings electronic ticket sale method is more popular to compare to traditional travel paper air ticket sale method.

However, online electronic ticket sale method has its disadvantages such as online transaction is unsafe, if the consumer 's name and address and visa card number is stolen to let any internet users to know to be used to buy any products from internet channel easily. Otherwise, traditional walk in offline travel paper ticket sale method is more safe, because the travel consumers can pay cash to the travel agents directly.

However, offline travel agent disadvantages include that the research identified that information communication and technology has very crucial role for tourism industry. Tourist can access any kind of information about tourism destination and tourism products from any part of the world. Tourism comprehends with social media. For example, it was found that (ICT) is bosting up tourism industry. (ICT) helps in searching the location, search for information on tourism products, and e-booking of airline tickets and hotel reservation.

The online travel sale service attraction is that the recent development in the field of information communication and technology and its practical application in tourism and hospitality industry. Generally , online travel sale service must have consumer side and the supplier side.

The decision making prcess of consumer was analyzed and it was found that travel information search and traveller individual electronic ticker pre paid to prebook any plane seat, hotel rooms and restaurants prices comparison to prebook service of traveler individual purchase behavior are corresponding with the usae of (ICT).

What is the online travel sale service strategy?

The two most important things for travel operators (agents) are online travel marketing and strategic management. Former can enhance business operations. Use of (ICT) develops financial capabilities , however, it depends on management choice, financial condition and position. Some researchers recommended that the usage of IT should not be restricted at operational level, however it should be extended up to senior level and should be used for decision making. Social media is regarded as a platform where the tourists and travel operators/agents (suppliers) of tourism industry cross each other. Thus, the role of social media has been directed for future research in tourism industry. Hence, it seems online travel sale service has these features to attract travel consumers to choose to use this online mode to buy electronic air ticket. Such as, airline electronic air ticket price comparison, pre-booking plan seats to avoid full seats flights to delay consumer individual trip plan, pre-booking hotel rooms and prices comparison as well as prebooking restaurant seats and food price and taste comparison, travel destination easy search. Otherwise, these features to attract travel consumers to choose to walk in to travel agents to buy paper air ticket directly. They include: safe cash or visa card payment to avoid personal information is stolen by website payment channel, e.g. via card number, address, name , birth date personal information. Also the travel consumer can enquire any questions from the travel agent and gets individual feedback from the travel agent by oral before who ensure to choose to buy which kind of travel package for whose travel destination. In special, when the travel consumer has much time to spend to enquire any travel trip question, walk in travel agent is the best enquire methods to let the travel consumer to know the trip information clearly.

● Online/offline travel operators (agents) maketing strategies
Offline walk in travel unique segment service strategy

Nowadays, online and offlce travel operators competitions are serious. In fact, tourism marketing , there will be more need for online travel operators in the future, due to online travel sale service is popular to be accepted by online travel consumers. Thus, I recommend walk in offline travel agents need to concentrate on focusing some unique travel service to attract new or old travel consumers if who hope to survive.

I recommend that they can focus on specific specialized services, such as travel consultation (specialization) hypothesizing that systematic differences exist between the usage of travel agents for different travel contexts and travel agents can survive if they focus on specific segments of the market, such as older travelers (segmentation; hypothesizing that systematic differences exist between the usage of travel agents depending on the personal characteristics of travellers). The unique travel needs include: specific services related to package holidays, transport services, beach on city holidays, as well as destinations travellers are not familiar with.

I shall give my opinions to provide insight into alternative strategies for travel agencies in a matured travel market with a high internet penetration as below:

The internet online travel sale service is a reality of popular to let travel consumers to feel convenient to pre-book air seat, hotel rooms , air electronic ticket prices comparison. In order to make final purchase decision very easily in the shortest time. Consequently , it has penetrated the decision making process of travel to attract them to choose to buy electronic air ticket, prebooking hotel rooms or restaurant seats from online travel agent channel more than walk in offline travel agent channel. This is especially true in the tourism business where consumption to consume (booking) and the purchase-related information search (Bieger & Lasesser 2004; Crotts 1998).

In fact , apply website to provide travel sale method has these good consequence. From travel operator (agent) supplier's perspective, the success potential derived from operating a website consist of lower distribution costs, higher revenues and a larger potential market share (due to the ubiquitous access). From traverler's perspective, the internet allows direct communication with tourism suppliers facilitatinf requests for information and allowing services and travel related products, e.g. prebooking hotel rooms, restaurant seats , electronic or paper air tickets, travel trip arrangement package products to be purchased at any time and any place from online travel agents /operators conveniently.

Offline / online travel agency (operator) business depends on earn commissions on behalf of airlines. Thus, offline walk in travel agency (operator) business model that would extend existence as a booking agency (thus focusing on consultation and interpersonal contact) strategy.

As a matter of fact, commission -cutting , which began in the US well ahed of Europe, has had a profound effect specially on business travel agents . Consequently , many of them have re-invented themselves as " travel managers", instead of selling tickets and making arrangements, they charge consultancy fees for reducing the amounts client companies spend on travel (Daneshku, 1999).

● Systematic differences strategy applies to offline walk in travel agent

Thus, I recommend systematic differences strategy can be applied offline walk in travel agent (operator). It means that walk in travel agents could reorient their offline walk in travel agent business to focus on contexts that are less substitutable by other channels and media . Factors hypothetically attributing to the delineation of travel contexts include: helping travellers to choose best travel destinations, helping travellers to attempt to find the number of previous trips (indicating the familiarity with a destination) for their travel reference, helping them to find the cheapest, the most convenient and the most close transportation to ctch during their trips, helping them to find the different types of accommodation and rooms price comparison , nature/type of the trip comparison , arrangement of time of booking (as indicator of spontneous / planned travel) nd helping them to budget overall travel expenditure .

Systematic differences in travel agent use exist in dependence of personal (characteristics with with tourists. Walk in offline travel agents could benefit from a travelling client segmentation strategy and customize and target their services to those travellers that are most likely to be and remain their customers.

Factors hypotheticlly attributing to the traveller segment include: travel expenditure per day, useful travel information as indicator for perceived risk and socio-demographic (age, gender, highest completed and education, professional positions) . Generally, the role of walk in offline travel agent with regard to the travel infrromation search and booking behavior have take an incoming perspective. Such as looking at visitors from different travel markets at a similar destinations. The comparison of central importance in determining whether specialization of travel contexts or market segments is the more promising strategy for walk in offline travel agents.

However, travel package tours strategy must b offline walk in travel attraction . Due to some walk in travellers target segmentation market has still needs. Generally, this travel package tours of travel segmentation consumer who like to enquire the travel agents to concern what the hotel rooms price are the cheapest to provide to them to live, what transportation tools the travel agent can arrange to them to catch anywhere the country destination, the travel agent can provide them to visit during their tour journey. Thus, the travel trip package service is still popular need to offline walk in travel agent (operator). This market is only belonged to offline walk in travel agents (operators) nowadays.

Service fees and commission cuts strategy

The reduction or removal of airline commission continues to challenge travel agencies' profitability It is crucial to understand what trends travel agencies need to be aware of to ensure how to profitability and increase travel agencies' revenues with service-fee models.

Service fees are not only a way to compensate for the loss of airline commission but also a way to generate new revenue sources for travel agencies that guarantee their long term profitability. Many travel agencies are expanding their service fee models, both in terms of the mounts changed and the number of service to airline.

However, if travel agent charge too much service fee to exceed the general airline travel market service fee reasonable or standard level. It will influence many airlines do not choose to find the travel agent to help them to sell air tickets. Travel agents apply fees most often for airline related services. They charge differentiated fees depending on the destination, type of reservation (e.g. frequent flyer), number of tickets sold or type of airline (e.g. full service versus).

However, service fee increases can raise customer loyalty and satisfaction. It won't reduce client numbers or result in a lose in clients.. The reason is that service fees can be tailored to suit individual customer. This helps travel agencies target their clients, with tailored services based on their past purchasing patterns and identity services for which clients' willingness to pay is greater , such as trip planning identity service for which pay , such as hotel only or special promotion.

To revenue mix for travel agencies is increasingly shifting to service fes as airlines have lowered or cut commissions. Successful travel agencies in many European countries are fast adopting, and constantly upgrading , their service fee schemes. Thus, it seems reasonable service fee level is one important factor to influence travel agents and airlines good relationship. In fact, even travel agents raise service fee, it won't influence travel consumer number to be reduced , even they raise air ticket price. It they can provide the informations concerning the reasonable hotel rooms prices and food quality comparison to satisfy travel consumers' living arrangement or helping them to find the reasonable restaurants' food prices and where are their location arrangement or providing the reasonable airlines' electronic air tickets or paper air tickets sale service, even arrangement any high entertainment quality of travel destination trips to let travel consumers to feel satisfactory.

However, I believe the raise air ticket price factor won't influence the travel consumer number to be decreased. Any offline or online travel agents will encounter this crisis. By cutting travel agents' commission. Airlines decreased their dependence on travel agencies as a distribution channel. In fact, three key variable factors will influence travel agents' commission income to be decreased. They include below:

● The unsustainable or no change financial losses by airlines , due to the growth of low cost carriers, leading to an increase in the number of bankruptcies.

● No negative consequences from previous commission cuts: airline had progressively lowed the commission payments.

● No effective resource for travel agencies to satisfy airlines needs.

● The appearance of now airlines and air routes to provide to travel agencies to fall down air ticket price to attract consumers' choices, due to who don't feel to spend much money to go to this new air routes or catch new airline plans , whether these new air routes are excite to entertainment or whether they are safe planes to catch.

● An increase in the number of bankruptcies to cause travel comsumption desire to be reduced.

● New competition forced down air fares.

● The necessity to cut production costs, especially with low cost meaning low production costs and low fares, even if the two are closely linked.

Internet negative influences to travel agents

Although, on the one hand, internet creates offline travel agents to use websites to help them to sell electronic air ticket or travel related products, such as prebooking hotel rooms , restaurants, transportation tools etc. travel service. However, on the other hand, internet also brings travel agencies competitive disadvantage with regad to suppliers' direct websites , when airlines are able to control seat availability and prices. Indeed internet cause the decision is made by the airlines to reduce and/or eliminate travel agency commission has led them to use technology that many of their distrust or are not inclined to use, and to compare prices and travel schedules constantly.

As a result of this travel sale service environment, traditional offline travel agencies are at a competitive disadvantage with regard to online travel agencie and to airline carriers, which have developed their own direct websites where they are able to control seat availability and prices.

Nevertheless, travel agents' pay programmes remain. From some airlines, travel agents receive negotiated incentive commission closely linked to their performance as incentive . However, airlines still need travel agents' assistance to help them to promote air tickets to sell, due to travel agents can provide trip packages, transportation tools, prebooking hotel rooms, restaurants and air tickets arrangement and they can give any enquiries to every individual travel consumer. It is free charge travel professional enquiry service for travel agency's competitive features.

Consequently, how agencies can reduce their reliance on airline commission payments. I recommend these following strategic options to them to apply as below:

● Streamlining operations, controlling staff costs, when ensuring the client feels as little impact as possible.

● Expanding or moving into the leisure business, where commissions on ono-air products remain high (cruise, hotel, railway travel)

● Specializing in geographic areas or becoming niche players for specific leisure products, e.g. destination weddings, student travel group cultural travel, cruises only, cruise and railway travel etc.

● (d) establishing a service fee driven business model.

Concentrating on business travel marketing strategy

The certain characteristics to the business travel market allowed this sector to adapt more easily to the disappearance of commission. Business travel systems have always had different relationship with different customers. They usually have long term buyer relationships, set up long before the commission cap. Some of them quickly renegotiated their contracts to include a transaction or management fee, knowing that the majority of these fee arrangements are specific the need of the client.

The reasons why airlines reduce commission to paid to travel agents. They include petrol costs increasing, e.g. indirect and by pass the established distribution chain by developing airlines' their own websites; reducing or removing commission paid to travel agencies. Consequently, the decision to cut travel agencies' commission clearly shows that airlines wanted to decrease their reliance and dependence on travel agencies as a distribution channel. Thus, the internet appears to be an efficient and cost-effective distribution channel. Also, by creating airlines' own websites and setting directly to their clients, airlines are also to control seat availability to their clients and prices to their websites.

What an e-commerce strategy is used by internet travel websites?

Nowadays, the commercial use of electronic travel ticket travel is common, the most purchased online products include, for example, the name brands in online travel Epedia.travel .com and cheap tickets have been or are being integrated in large online travel firms.

Generally, online travel websites apply these strategies to attract travel consumers as below:

Firstly, shopping mall strategy, means to conduct a comprehensive factors for e-commerce. The online service provider needs to organize catalogs of services, take orders through their websites, accept payments securely, send service or related document, such as airline tickets to consumers and manage client data , such as client profiles.

Secondly, portal strategy, portal websites , such as yahoo give visitors the chance to find almost everything , they are working for in one place. Websites , such as Altavista.com and yahoo.com provide users with a shopping page that links them to many sites carrying a variety of products. Once a client is familiar with a website, who will be more likely to use the online service.

Thirdly, pricing strategy, low price is as a major competitive weapon. It includes a comparison pricing on discount price or price negotiation to let online travel consumers to get the best electronic travel ticket price choice to buy any airline tickets.

Travel agents vs online booking: Tackling the shortcomings and strengths

Consequently, however, one travel consumer who chooses either online booking sale service or traditional walk in offline travel agent to enquire travel service. These both of travel sale methods have shortcomings also. Such as it is possible that online electronic travel ticket purchase has personal data ,e.g. visa card, name, birth data, address, which will be stolen by online crime internet users more easily, who can not enquire any travel questions to get clear travel information concern whose travel destination package service choice or hotel room choice or transportation tool or restaurant choice and airline choice by travel agent. Also, it is possible that walk in travel agent paper travel ticket purchase shortcomings include that the travel consumer can not check any airlines' seat and pre book hotel room or transport tool or restaurant in the shorten time if who needs to fly immediately. Thus, it seems that online travel agent's client group is business travel intention, who does not need to enquire travel agent and has desire to per book airline seat in the short time. Otherwise, the offline walk in agent's client group is entertainment intention , who need to walk in to travel agent to enquire whose travel package and has no desire to pre book airline seat in the short time. Thus, online travel agent ought concentrate on design good travel package for the business travel consumers. Otherwise, offline travel agent ought concentrate on design good travel package for the entertainment travel consumers. Thus, they can have themselves unique travel target package to adopt to their different travel need. Such as business travel consumers need to live cheap and comfortable hotels, catching cheap and fast transportation tools in their business trips, eating in cheap and good taste food in restaurant and spending the less time to catch the airline plan to arrive the destination and cheap and comfortable business class plan seat. Such as entertainment travel consumers need the travel agent can help them to design cheap and enjoyable travel package, includes living comfortable hotel room, exciting and enjoyable trip, good taste food and

railway, travel bus, cruise and plane provision in trip.

In conclusion, In fact, tourism is a quite unique area of business in a sense that is a travel sale service product and it can't be observed or manipulated through direct experience prior to purchase . Instead clients have to purely rely on indirect or virtual experience. Thus, every online or offline travel agent ought attempt to design different travel package to attract every business traveler or entertainment traveller trip need because every traveler will have personal unique trip need in this competitive travel sale service market in the future.

Reference

Bieger. Th., and Ch. Laesser (2004). " Information sources for travel decisions: Toward a source process model," Journal of travel reserch, 42(4): 357-371.

Daneshku, S. (1999). " Unwived travel agents unworried bi internet, " Financial Times , London. June 16, 1999:10.

Foucault, B. Lery, N. Rifkin, A. & Silfies , 2000.
" Comparision of textbook prices by retailer and by college" working paper. Cornell University, Ithaca, Ney.

CHAPTER THREE

Traveler past travel experience

Prediction travel behavioral consumption from traditional human's mind of tourism market research method

How to predict travel consumption? It is one question to any travel agents concern to use what methods which can predict how many numbers of travelers where who will choose to go to travel more accurately. I think that who can consider how to predict travel behavioral consumption from psychology view and computer science view both.

On the psychology view, It has evidence to support the relationship between self-identify threat and resistance to change travel behavior to any travelers, controlling for whose past travelling behavior, resistance to change if a psychological phenomenon of long standing interest in many applied branches of psychology. Past travelling behavior has been acknowledged as a predictor of future action. Such as travelling behavior that is experienced as successful is likely to be repeated and may lead to habitual patterns. Some psychologists differentiate habit between two concepts, such as goal oriented and automatic oriented both. Although repeated past travelling behavior is addition goal oriented and automatic oriented. Further non-deliberative nature of habit may make appeals to judge and to predict future individual traveler's behaviour accrately. However, repeated travelling behavior without a necessary constraint of goal orientation and automatic oriented both. So, it seems that psychological factor can influence any individual traveler why and how who choose to decide whose travelling behaviour.

On the computer statistic view, structural equation modeling is an extremely flexible linear-in-parameters multivariate statistical modeling technique. It has been used in modeling travel behavior and values since about 1980 year. It is a software method to handle a large number of variables, as well as unobserved variables specified as linear combinations (weighted averages) of the observed variable.

Whether climate change can influence travelling behaviours.

The flexibility of human travelling behavior is at least the result of one such mechanism, our ability to travel mentally in time and entertain potential future. Understanding of the impacts is holidays, particularly those involving travel. Using focus groups research to explores tourists' awareness of the impacts of travel own climate change, examines the extent to which climate change features in holiday travel decisions and identifies some of the barriers to the adoption of less carbon intensive tourism practices. The findings suggest many tourists don't consider climate change when planning their holidays. The failure of tourists to engage with the climate change to impact of holidays, combined with significant barriers to behavioral change, presents a considerable challenge in the tourism industry.

Tourism is a highly energy intensive industry and has only recently attracted attention as an important contributions to climate change through greenhouse gas emissions. It has been estimated that tourism contributes 5% of global carbon dioxide emissions. There have been a number of potential changes proposed for reducing the impact of air travel on climate change. These include technological changes, market based changes and behavioral changes. However, the role that climate change plays in the holiday and travel decisions of global tourists. How the global tourists of the impacts travel has on climate change to establish the extent to which climate change, considerations features in holiday travel decision making processes and to investigate the major barriers to global tourists adopting less carbon intensive travel practices. Whether tourists will aware the impacts that their holidays and travel have on climate changes.

When, it comes to understand indvidual traveler's behavioral change, wide range of conceptual theories have been developed, utilizing various social, psychological, subjective and objective variables in order to model travel consumption behavior. These theories of travel behavioral change operate at a number of different levels, including the individual level, the interpersonal level and community level. Whether pro-environmental behavior can be used to predict travel consumption behavior in a climate change. However, the question of what determines pro-environmental behavior in such a complex one that it can not be visualized through one single framework or diagram.

Despite the potentially high risk scenario for the tourism industry and the global environment, the tourism and climate change ought have close relationship. Whether what are the important factors and variables which can limit tourism? e.g. money, time, family problem, extreme hot or cold weather change, air ticket price, journey attraction etc. variable factors. Mention of holidays and travel were deliberately avoided in the recruitment process, so as not to create a connection factor to influence traveler's individual mind. However, the dismissal of alternative transportation modes can be conceived as either a structural barrier, in the sense that flying is perhaps the only realistic option to reach long-haul holiday destination, or a perceived behavioral control barriers in that an individual perceives flying as the only option open to whom. The transportation tool factor will be depend to extent on the distance to the destination. This can also be interpreted in a social perspective as an intention with the resources available where much international tourism is structured around flying. To increase the availability of different transportation modes, tourists could choose holiday destination closer to home.

Finally, also how to predict future travel behavioural consumption. I feel that travel agents need to predict whether any country's random daily variation of weather factor is also important to influence travel behaviour. e.g. in weather, temperature, rainfall adn snowfall with traffic accidents factors will have relationship to cause travel demand. Some scientists estimate suggest that when warmed temperatures and reduced snowfall are associated with a moderate decline in non-fatal accidents, they are also associated with a significant increase in fatal accidents. Thus increase in fatalities and temperature. Half of the estimated effect of temperature on fatalities is due to changes in the exposure to pedestrians, bicyclists and motorcyclists as temperature increase. So, if any countries have rainfall, snowfall and low temperature to cause traffic accidents, whether this accident occurrence will influence the travelers who liking climb snow hills, riding bicycle, running sports who will avoid to travel to these countries' bad weather after occurs. So, why I feel that this natural climate factor will also be one serious factor to influence travel behavioral consumption.

Market method predicts future travel consumption behavior

Whether individual habitual behaviour can influence travelling behaviour : e.g. renting travel transportation tools

Whether habit can be intended to predict of future travel behavior to people are creatures of habits. Many of human's everyday goal-directed behaviors are performed in a habitual fashion, the transportation made and route one takes to work, one's choice of breakfast. Habits are formed when using the some behavior frequently and a similar consistency in a similar context for the some purpose whether the individual past travel consumption model will be caused a habit to whom. e.g. choosing whom travel agent to buy air ticket or traveling package; choosing the same or similar countries' destinations to go to travel ; choosing the business class or normal (general) class of quality airlines to catch planes. Does habitual rent traveling car tools use not lead to more resistance to change of travel mode? It has been argued that past behavior is the best predictor of future behavior to travel consumption. If individual traveler's past consumption behavior was always reasoned, then frequency of prior travel consumption behavior should only have an indirect link to the individual traveler's behavior. It seems that renting travel car tools to use is a habit example. So, a strong rent traveling car tools useful habit makes traveling mode choice. People with a strong renting of traveling car tools of habit should have low motivation to attend to gather any information about public transportation in their choice of travelling country for individual or family or friends members during their traveling journeys.

Even when persuasive communication changes the traveler whose attitudes and intention, in the case of individual traveler or family travelers with a strong renting travel car tools habit. It is difficult to change whose travel behaviors to choose to catch public transportation in whose any trips in any countries. However, understanding of travel behavior and the reasons for choosing one mode of transportation over another. The arguments for rent traveling car tools to use, including convenience, speed, comfort and individual freedom and well known. Increasingly, psychological factors include such as, perceptions, identity, social norms and habit are being used to understand travel mode choice. Whether how many travel consumers will choose to rent traveling car tools during their trips in any countries. It is difficult to estimate the numbers. As the average level of renting travel car tools of dependence or attitudes to certain travel package policies from travel agents. Instead different people must be treated in different ways because who are motivated in different ways and who are motivated by different travel package policies ways from travel agents.

In conclusion, the factors influence whose traveler's individual behavior either who chooses to rent traveling car tools or who chooses to catch public transportation when who individual goes to travel in alone trip or family trip. It include influence mode choice factors, such as social psychology factor and marketing on segmentation factor both to influence whose transportation choice of behavior in whose trip.

How to determine future travel behavior from past travel experience and perceptions of risk and safety for the benefits to travel consumers?

How to determine future travel behavior from past travel experience and perceptions of risk and safety for the benefits to travel consumers? Why does individual traveler avoid certain destination(s) is(are) as relevant to tourist decision making as why who chooses to travel to others. Perceptions of risk and safety and travel experience are likely to influence travel decisions. If travel agents had efforts to predict future travel behavior to guess whether travelers will feel where is(are) risk and unsafe to cause who does not choose to go to the country to travel. Then, the travel agents will avoid to choose to spend much time to design the different traveling package to attract their potential travel consumers to choose to travel. The reason is because in the case of individual traveler's tourism experience, the traveler whose past disappointment travel experience (psychological risk) will be a serious threat to the traveler's health or life (health, physical or terrorism risk). The past safety or unhealthy risk to the country(countries) will influence the traveler decides to choose not to go to the countries(country) to travel again in the future.

What is push and pull factors to influence any traveler who chooses where is whose preferable travelling destination

How to predict individual traveler's behavioral intention of choosing a travel destination. Understanding why people travel and what factors influence their behavioral intention of choosing a travel destination is beneficial to tourism planning and marketing. In general, an individual's choice of a travel destination into two forces. The first force is the push factor that pushes an individual away from home and attempt to develop a general desire to go somewhere, without specifying where that may be. The other force is the pull factor that pull an individual toward in destination, due to a region-specific or perceived attractiveness of a destination. The respective push and pull factors illustrate that people travel because who are pushed by whose internal motives and pulled by external forced of a destination. However, the decision making process leading to the choice of a travel destination is a very complex process. For example, a Taiwanese traveler who might either choose new travel destination of Hong Kong or another old travel Asia destinations again or who also might choose any one of Western country, as a new travel destination. The travel agents can predict where who will have intention to choose to travel from whose past behavior and attitude, subjective and perceived behavioral control model.

The factors influence where is the traveler choice, include personal safety, scenic beauty, cultural interest, climate changing, transportation tools, friendliness of local people, price of trip, trip package service in hotels and restaurants, quality and variety of food and shopping facilities and services etc. needs. So, whose factors will influence where is the individual travel's choice. It seems every traveler whose choice of travel process, will include past behavior. e.g. travelling experience, travelling habit, then to choose the best seasoned travelling action to satisfy whose travel needs. This process is the individual traveler's psychological choice process, who must need time to gather information to compare concerning of different travel packages, destination scene, climate change, transportation tools available to the destination, air ticket price etc. these factors, then to judge where is the best right destination to travel in the right time.

Why expectation, motivation and attitude factor can influence travelling behaviour.

Social psychology is concerned with gaining insight into the psychological of socially relevant behaviors and the processes. For instance, on a global level bad influence to global warming, it influences some countries extreme cold or hot bad climate changing occurrence, then it ought influence some travelers' behavioral decision to change their mind to choose some countries to go to travel at the moment which do not occur extreme hot or cold climate (temperature). e.g. above than 40 degree in summer or below than 0 degree in winter. Due to the extreme climate changing environment in the countries, it will cause them to feel uncomfortable to play during their trips. So, the global warming causes to climate changing factor will influence the numbers of travel consumption to be reduced possibly. This is global climate changing environment factor influences to bad or uncomfortable social psychological feeling to global travelers' mind of traveling decision. What is individual traveler expectation, motivation and attitude? Tourism sector includes inbound (domestic) tourism and outbound (overseas) tourism both incomes to any countries. According to recent article, a tourist behavior model has been developed, called the expectation, motivation and attitude (EMA) model (Hsu et al., 2010).

This model focuses on the pre-visit stage of tourists by modeling the behavioral process by incorporating expectation, motivation and attitude. Travel motivation is considered as an essential component of the behavioral process, which has been increasing attention from the travel; industry. The economic approach defines "tourism" is an identifiable nationally important industry. It includes the component activities of transportation, accommodation, recreation, food and related service. So, tourism behavioral consumption is concerned the individual tourist's usual habituate of the industry which responds to whose needs, and of the impacts that both the tourist and the tourism industry have on the socio-cultural, economic and physical environment.

However, travel motivation means how to understand and predict factors that influence travel decision making. According to Backman and others (1995, p.15), motivation is conceptually viewed as " a state of need, a condition that services as a driving force to display different kind of behavior toward certain types of activities, developing preferences, arriving at some expected satisfactory outcome." So, motivation and expectancy which has close relationship to any tourist before who decided to do any tourism of behavior. Some economists confirmed motivation and expectancy which has relations, such as expectation of visiting an outbound destination has a direct effect on motivation to visit the destination; motivation has a direct effect on attitude toward visiting the destination; expectation of visiting the outbound destination has a direct affect on attitude toward visiting the destination and motivation has a mediating effect on the relationship in between expectation and attitude.

What methods can predict future travel behavioural consumption

How to use qualitative of travel behavioural method to predict future travel consumption?

I also suggest to use qualitative of travel behavioural method to predict future travel consumption. Methods such as focus groups interviews and participant observer techniques can be used with quantitative approaches on their own to fill the gaps left by quantitative techniques. These insights have contributed to the development of increasingly sophisticated models to forecast travel behavior and predict changes in behavior in response to change in the transportation system. First, survey methods restrict not only the question frame but the answer frame as well, anticipating the important issues and questions and the responses. However, these surveys methods are not well suited to exploratory areas of research where issues remain unidentified and the researched seek to answer the question "why?". Second, data collection methods using traditional travel diaries or telephone recruitment can under represent certain segments of the population, particularly the older persons with little education, minorities and the poor. Before the survey, focus group for example can be used to identify what socio-demographic variables to include in the survey, how best to structure the diary, even what incentives will be most effective in increasing the response rate. After the survey, focus, focus groups can be used to build explanations for the survey results to identify the "why" of the results as well as the implications. One Asia Pacific survey research result was made by tourism market investigation before. It indicated the travel in Asia Pacific market in the past, had often been undertaken in large groups through leisure package sold in bulk, or in large organized business groups, future travelers will be in smaller groups or alone, and for a much wider range of reasons. Significant new traveler segments, such as female business traveler. The small business traveler and the senior traveler, all of which have different aspirations and requirements from the travel experience.

Moreover, Asia tourism market will start to exist behaviors in the adoption of newer technologies, a giving the traveler new ways to manage the travel experience, creating new behaviors. This with provide new opportunities for travel providers. The use of mobile devices, smartphones, tablets etc. and social media are the obvious findings to become an integral part of the travel experience. Thus, quality method can attempt to predict Asia Pacific tourism market development in the future.

However, improving the predictive power of travel behavior models and to increase understanding travel behavior which lies in the use of panel data(repeated measures from the same individuals). Whereas, cross-sectional data only reveal inter-individual differences at one moment in time, panel data can reveal intra-individual changes over time. In effect, panel data are generally better suited to understand and predict (changes in) travel behavior. However, a substantial proportion was also observed to transition between very different activity/travel patterns over time, indicating that from one year to the next, many people renegotiated their activity/travel patterns.

How to apply advanced traveler information systems (ATIS) to predict future travelling behaviour?

Nowadays, information can impact on traveler behavior and network performance. For example, when steadily growing levels of vehicle ownership and vehicle miles traveled information has been identified as a potential strategy towards man aging travel demand, optimizing transportation networks and better utilizing available capacity. Toward, this goal to predict further tourist behavioral consumption. Many countries, government tourism development institutes has applied advanced traveler information systems (ATIS) which travel behavior models and high-fidelity network performance models made increasingly feasible through the rapid advances in computer power. Crucial components of this problem domain are the modeling of individual tourist drivers' response to travel information and the development accurate guidance of relevance to real would trip makers. So, this advanced traveler information systems (ATIS) can assist the tourist who like to rent travelling car tools to travel in any countries own free traveler information systems service conveniently. Also, this travel information system can be intended to assist travelers to make better travel choices. e.g. this system can improve the decision making of individual traveler rather than improvements of network performance overall. So, we need to understand how tourists make their travel plans. Also, understanding decision process that lead to booking of the trip is equally important, as it allows of a potential behavior.

How does online tourism sale channel can influence traveling consumption of behaviour?

Nowadays, internet is popular, it seems that booking air ticket behavior of using internet is predicted to influence overall tourism air tickets payment method. Tourism industry has grown in the previous several decades. Despite its global impact, questions related to better understanding of tourists and whose habits. Using online travel air ticket booking benefits include booking electronic air tickets can be made from entering any electronic travel agents websites in the short time and electronic travel ticket payers do not need leave home, who can pay visa card to pre booking any electronic travel ticket from online channel conveniently.

How to analyze activity based travel demand ? Nowadays, human are concerning the traffic congestion and air quality deterioration, the supply oriented focus of transportation planning has expanded to include how to manage travel demand within the available transportation supply. Consequently, there has been an increasing interest in travel demand management strategies, such as congestion pricing that attempts to change aggregate travel demand. The prediction aggregate level, long term travel demand to understanding disaggregate level (i.e. individual levels) behavioral responses to short term demand policies, such as ride sharing incentives, congestion pricing and employer based demand management schemes, alternate work schedules, telecommuting limitation of travel agent traditionally work nature shall influence oriented trip based travel modelling passenger travel demand indirectly.

Finally, online travel purchase will be popular to influence the number of travel behavioural consumption nowadays. Any travel package products can be sold from websites to attract travellers to choose to prebook air ticket for any trips conveniently. In the past ten years, the internet has become the predominant carrier of all types of information and transactions. Regarding travel decisions, internet has also become an important sales channels for the travel industry, because it is associated with comparably lower distribution and sales costs, but also because ir adapts to hign supply and demand dynamics in this industry. Consequently, the travel and tourism industry tries to increase the internet sale specific share of sales volumes. So, internet sale channel has changed travel consumption behavioural pattern and characteristics and travel experience. For example, Switzerland has one of the highest population-to-computer ratio in Europe. It is also one of the most highly internet penetrated countries in terms of use of the WWW on a day-to-day basis, with more than 75 percent of the population older than 14 years using the WWW daily (ICT, 2005).

The reason of booking online tourism may include: convenience, fast transaction, finding traveling package choice easily, more airline seats available. So, online booking tourism will influence the traditional tourism agents visiting of sales and air tickets and travelling package numbers to be decreased. Finally, the online booking tourism market shares will be expanded to more than traditional tourism agents visits sale market in the future one day. So, the travel agents who still use the traditional tourism visiting sale channel which ought raise whose features to compare to differ to online tourism sale channel if these traditional touriam agents want to keep competitive ability in tourism industry for long term.

Actively based patterns of urban population of travel behavioural prediction method.

Actively based patterns of urban population. It is a method of motivational framework means in which societal constraints and inherent individual motivations interact to shape activity participation patterns. It can be used to predict one city or urban the numbers of travel demand in the year. It has two elements: First, capability constraints refer to constraints are imposed by biological needs, such as eating and sleeping and/or resources, such as income, availability of cars etc. to undertake the urban or city's family activities in the year. Second, coupling constraints define where, when and the duration of planning activities that are to be pursued with other individuals. So, this method needs to gather information (data) to get the relationship between activities, travel and spending work time and space time to evaluate whether there are how many families who have real needs to spend time to go to travel in the year.

What is trip based versus activity based approaches?

What is trip based versus activity based approaches? The fundamental difference between the trip-based and activity based approaches is that the former approach directly focuses on trips without explicit recognition of the motivation or reason for the trips and travel. The activity based approach , on the other hand, views travel as a demand derived from the need to pursue travel activities. So, it is better understand the individual or family behavior basis for individual or family travelling decision regarding participation in travelling activities in certain places or cities or countries at given times and hence the resulting travel needs. This behavioral basis includes all the factors that influence the why, how, when and where of performed activities and resulting individuals and household, the cultural/social norms of the community and the travel surrounding environment.

Another difference between the two approaches is in the way travel is represented. The trip based approach represents travel as a collection of trips. Each trip is considered as independent of other trips, without considering the inter-relationship in the choice attributes , such as time, destination and mode of different trips. As tours are chains of trips beginning and ending at a same location , say home or work. The tour based representation helps maintain the consistency across and capture the interdependency and consistency of the modeled choice attributed among the trips of the same tour.

In addition to the tour based representation of travel, the activity based approach focuses on sequences or patterns of activity participation and travel behavior, using the whole day or longer periods of time is the unit of analysis. Such as approach can address travel demand management issues through an examination of how people modify their activity participation, for example, will individuals substitute more out-of-home activities for in home activities in the evening of who arrived early form work due-to a work schedule change?

The major difference between trip based and the activity based approaches is in the way, the time dimension of activities and travel is considered. In the trip based approach, time is reduced to being simply a cost making a trip and a day's viewed as a combination, defined peak and off peak time periods. On the other hand, activity based approach views individuals' activity travel patterns are a result of their time use decisions with a continuous time domain. As individuals have 24 hours in a day or multiples of 24 hours for longer periods of time and decide how to use that travel among or allocate that time to activities and travel and with who, subject to their socio-demographic, transportation system and other and scheduling of trips. So, determining the impact of travel demand management policies on time use behavior is an important step to assessing the impact of such policies on individual travel behavior. The final major difference between this two approaches relates to the level of aggregation. In the trip based approach, most aspect of travel, e.g. number of trips etc. are analyzed at an aggregate level. Consequently, trip based methods accommodate the effect of socio-demographic attributes of households and individuals in a very limited fashion, which limits the activity of the method to evaluate travel impacts of long term socio-demographic characteristics of the individuals who actually make the activity travel choices and the travel service characteristics of the surrounding environment. So, the activity based models are better equipped to forecast the longer term changes in travel demand in response composition and the travel environment of urban areas. Also, using activity based models, the impact of policies can be assessed by predicting individual level behavioral responses instead of employing trip based statistical averages that are aggregated over defined demographic segments.

Why senior age will be main travelling target?

In the past, Germany government had established tourism survey analysis to analyze survey data in order to arrive at reliable conclusions on future trends in travel behavior. To aim to find how demographic change will influence the tourism market and how the industry can adapt to those changes. The travel analysis provided data on tourism consumer behavior, including attitudes, motives and intentions. Since, 1970 year, it is based on a random sample, representative for the population in private households aged 14 years or older. Then, a continuous high scientific standard combined with a national and international users makes the travel analysis a useful tool and reliable source for tourism industry and policy decisions. It aimed to gather statistical data. e.g. on the age structure and on demographic trends, quantitative and qualitative analysis with time series data from the travel analysis. It shows e.g. not only the future volume , quite different from today's seniors, or how who will travel of family holidays will change, e.g. single parents of low, but grandparents of growing significance for tourism.

Demographic change is said to be one of the important drivers for new trends in consumer traveling change behavior in most European countries (e.g. Lind 2001). Because the growing number of senior citizens in the European Union and other industralised countries, such as the USA and Japan, looks to become one of the major marketing challenges for the tourism industry. United Nations statistics predict that the share of people being 60 age or older will grow dramatically in the coming future, and is expected to rise from 10 percent of the world population in 2000 year to more than 20 percent in 2050 year (United Nations Population Division, 2001). From its statistic, some data showed that travel propensity increased throughout life until the age of about 50 years of age and was then kept stable until very late in life 75 age. The most important results is that the travel propensity when getting older is not going down between 65 and 75 age of course, the overall development of this variable is influenced by a lot of other factors which are rsponsible for quite a variation over time. It is now possible to suggest that the general pattern of travel propensity is one of the key indicators for holiday life cycle travel behaviour, includes three stages. The growth stage tends to increase from early aduithood until 45 age old or when reaching some 80%. The next stage is stabilisation from the ages of around 50 age,until 75 age old, starting with a lower increase. Finally, the decrease stage is a slight decrease occurs once people reach the more advanced age of 75 age to 85 age old (Lohmann & Danielsson 2001).

So, it seems Germany government tourism prediction to future travellers' behaviour indicated these findings, such as on how future senior generations will travel, who had used survey data to examine the patterns of travel behaviour of a generation getting older and applied the findings to draw conclusions on the future.

Also, it predicted that on the future of family trips, family semgmentation will be the travel behaviour patterns in the future. These findings together with the statistical data on demographic change allowed for a better understanding of the coming tends in family holidays. It's aim developed in consumer behaviour related to demographic change and predicted what will happen future of tourism one had to consider other influences and drivers as well, for example, trends on the supply side. e.g. low cost airlines or in travelling consumption behaviour in general whether how the past may provide a key to predict travel patterns of senior sitizens to the future.

Given the projected growth of the senior citizens market, designing specific marketing strategies to meet the prospective needs of elderly tourists will become increasingly important. It has been an implict assumption that it will be a close relationship between the travel behaviour of today's senior citizens and the those of future ones. The growing number of senior citizens in the world. e.g. China, Hong Kong, Japan, USA etc. countries. Global senior citizen tourism market will be based solely on demographic predictions about the future of the population's age structure. However, many of these seniors won't only live longer but will be fitter and more active until later in life. Many of the will also have plenty in life. Many of them will also have plenty of time and money to spend on travel. So, will these new seniors behave like today's senior citizens? Will they adopt the same travel behaviour as the previous generation or become a new market of oldies for the leisure and tourism indudtry? However, to determine the actual number of senior citizens who will be travelling and to sought to evaluate and specify certain difficult to predict the actual numbers of senior citizen to any country. However, they can be based on the implicit assumption that there is a close relationship between the travel behaviour of past, present and future seniors. But is this a valid assumption? As the reiseanalyse travel analysis survey, which was conducted in Germany every year, offered some interesting data possibiltieis. It was designed to monitor the holiday travel behaviour, opinions and attitudes of Germans and has been carried out since 1970 year, questions in the questionnaire. Data are based on face to face interviews, with a representative sample of more than 7,500 repondents, the interviews being carried out in January each year. All results refer to the average for the defined generated, which ranges generally over ten years. The group of people then at the age of 60 to 69 age is described. This corresponds to the same generation ten years ago, when they had an age of 50 to 59 age. When this methodological approach is not necessarily very sophisticated, it does have the important advantages of being cost effective.

Psychological method to predict travel behavioural consumption.

On the psychological view point, I think individual traveler's character will have those kind of personal characteristics. First, simplicity searchers value above everything ease not transparency in their travel planning and holiday making, and are willing to avoid having to go through extensive research. Second, cultural purists use their travel as an opportunity to immerse themselves in an unfamiliar looking to break themselves entirely from their home lives and engage. Sincerely with a different way of living. Third, social capital seekers understand that to be well travelled is a personal quality, and their choices are shaped by their desire to take maximum of social reward from their travel. They will exploit the potential of digital media to enrich and inform their experiences, and structure their adventures always keeping in mind they are being watched by online audiences. Finally, reward hunters seek a return on the investment who make in their busy , high-achieving lives. Linked in part to the growing trend of wellness, including both physical and mental self improvement who seek truly extraordinary and often indulgent or luxurious' must have experiences.

Why needs to know the personal character of individual traveler's characteristics? Because if travel agents could feel which kinds of individual traveler's character, then who can predict which kind of travel package to design to them more easily. For example, how to determine future travel behaviour from past travel experience and perceptions of risk and safety? We need to concern that the influences of past international travel experience, types of risk associated with international travel and the overall degree of safety feeling during international travel on individual's travelling experiences likelihood of travelling to various geographic regions on their next international vacation trip or avoidance of those regions, due to perceived risk. Because individual traveler's experience of safety risk degree to the countries, it will influence who chooses to go to the countries/country to travel again.

Why do travellers avoid certain destinations are as relevant decision making? Why do they choose to go to the country(countries) to travel? Perceptions of risk and safety and travel experiences are likely to influence travel decisions; efforts to predict future travel behaviour can benefit to individual tourist's decision making. As Weber & Bottorn (1989) defined risky decision is as "choices among alternatives that can be described by prodability distributions over possible outcomes" (p.114). Some psychologists judge subjective perceptions of physical reality, i.e. image of a particular tourist destination, whereas value judgement refers to the way individual rank destinations according to whose attributes. i.e. attractiveness, safety, risk etc. factors to form on overall image. So, if the individual traveler had unhappy and worried and unsafe experiences to go to where the place(country) to travel during whose vacation time before. Then, this negative travel experience will influence who is afraid to go to the place (country) to travel again. Risk of place, country, destination or region means the danger is relatively high to the place, ie. increasing in airplane accidents, crime or terrorist activity targeting citizens of potential traveler's nationality or the probability of occurrence is great , ie. recent occurrences involving travel regions/destinations under consideration or effective actions to control consequences exist. i.e. selecting safe regions and destinations, taking extra precautions when traveling to risky destinations. These risk factors will influence the individual traveler who chooses to cancel travel plan to go to the country again.

Another interesting research, how to predict behavioural intention of choosing a travel destination, which has focus of toursm research for years, but the complex decision making process leading to the choice of a travel destination has not been well researched. The planned behaviour model using its core constructs, attitude, subjective norm and perceived behavioural control, with the addition of the past behavioural variable on behavioural intention of choosing a travel destination.

Understanding why people travel and what factors influence their behavioural intention of choosing a travel destination is beneficial to tourism planning and marketing. Understanding travel motivation is the push and pull model. The idea of the push and pull model is the decomposition of an individual's choice of a travel destination into two forces. The first force is the push factor that pushes an indvidual away home and attempts to develop a general desire to go somewhere else, without specifying where that may be. The second force is the pull factor, that pulls on individual toward a destination, due to a region specific travel location or perceived attractiveness of a destination. The respective push and pull factors illustrate that people travel because who are pushed by their internal motives and pulled by external forces of a destination. Nevertheless, how push and pull factors guide people's attitude and how these attributes lead to behavioural intentions of choosing a travel destination have rarely been investigated. The decision making process leading to the choice of a travel destination is a very complex process. The planned behaviour model is as a research framework to predict the behavioural intention of choosing a travel destination. The model based on the three constructs of attitude, subjective norm, and perceived behavioural control (Fishbein & Ajzen, 1975).

In conclusion, the factors can influence travelers who decide to choose to travel the country, which include personal safety was perceived to the highest motivation factors among the important factors which include, scenic beauty, cultural interests, friendliness of local people, price of trip, services in hotels and restaurants, quality and variety of food and shopping facilities and services. The factors include both push and pull. Push factors include knowledge, prestige, and enhancement of human relationship etc., whereas, the most significant pull factors include high technologic image, expenditure and accessibility etc. For example, Japanese travelers visiting Hong Kong. Push factors are such as exploration dream fulfillment and pull factors are such as benefits sought, attractions and good climate city. It will be the factor of future travel patterns and motivations of sub-cultural and ethic groups for Japanese choice to go to Hong Kong travelling.

Bibliography

Backman, K., Backman, S., Uysal, M. And Sunshine, K. (1995). Event Tourism : An Examination Of Motivations And Activities. Festival Management And Event Tourism, 3(1), 15-24.

Fishbein, M., & Ajzen, Z. (1975). Belief, Attitude, Intention And Behaviour: An Introduction To Theory And Research, Boston: Addison Wesley.

Hsu, C.H.C., Cai , L.A., Li, M(2010). Expectation, Motivation And Attitude: A Tourist Behavioral Model. Journal Of Travel Research, 49(3), 282-296. http://dx.doi, org/10.1177/004728750 9349266.

ICT Information And Communication Technology Switzerland, 2005. ICT Fakten (ICT facts). Available from http://www.ictswitzerland.ch/de/ict%2fakten/factsfigures.asp(retrieved Dec.12, 2005) in German.

Lind, (2001): Befolkningen, Familjen, Livscykeln- Och Ekonomisk Tillvaxt. Institutet For Tillvaxtpo-litiska studier/Vinnova/Nutek.

Lohmann, Martin (2001): The 31 st. Reiseanalyse-RA 2001. Tourism: vol. 49, no.1/2001;pp.65-67, Zagreb.

United Nations Population Division (2001). World Population

Prospects: The 2000 year Revision, New York.
Weber E.U., & W, P.Bottom (1989). "Axiomatic
Measures Of Perceived Risk: Some Tests And extensions." journal
of behavioral decision making, 2 (2): 113-31.

CHAPTER FOUR

New economic development influences tourism needs

● How to develop new economic tourism industry

How to develop tourism industry in new economic environment? Any examination of the new economic development of travel and tourism requires definitions of the subject and its components, which are suitable for economic analysis. However, in new economic development to tourism industry, it is also important to look at tourism conceptually, in order to set the scene for a deeper understanding of the future new tourism industry development.

Tourism is neither a phenomenon nor a simple set if industries, however, in new or old economic development environment. It is a human activity which encompasses human behavior, use of resources, and interaction with other people, economies and leisure enjoyment environment. It is also involved physical movement of tourists to locales other than their normal living places.

In future new economic environment, traditional travel needs to include these element in order to satisfy traveler enjoyment and leisure feeling: They may include: Tourist needs and motivations, tourism selection and behavior and constraints , travel away from home , market interactions between tourists and those supplying products to satisfy tourist needs and impacts on tourists , hosts, economies and environments.

In new economic environment, the tourism products may include: carriers, in any forms of transport for tourist travel accommodation, man-made attractions, which could also include the managed areas of natural attractions, private sector and public sector support services, middlemen, such as tour wholesalers and travel agents.

The tourism resources may also include: Natural resources, lands , minerals, water and biological; labor resources, human work, and enterprise; capital resources, manmade enhancement and other resources. The travel and tourism resources problems may include: As there is frequently a mismatch between producer and consumer perception of what constitutes the tourism product , there may be conflict in ideas of which resources are properly involved as well as many of the resources likely to be in demand for tourism are public goods , or even free resources.

In new economic development to tourism industry view, we need to consider that tourism and travel has the reputation of being a relatively clean and pleasant industry in which to work or invest in order to attract a greater number of resource suppliers than as less well-perceived industry, which therefore keeps rewards prices down by competition, how to attract those retiring from or travel business for example, if their finances are already sound, income from travel is not expected to be optimal , travel and tourism is frequently highly seasonal , offering rewards that are competitive with other industries only some of the time, destination products are often in locations which are of little use to other industries, so that competition for resource use if minimal and hence rewards are low.

In general, tourist purpose may include: recreational purpose : holiday, health and sport and religion as well as business purpose: company business , e.g. conventions and sales trips. So, in new economic tourism development aim, tourism industry need consider hoe to achieve incentive trips to let these both tourists to feel. For example, the overall type of tourism required, destination arrangement, travel mode, accommodation and attraction visiting and purchasing method or distribution channel. The purchasing method choices may include: whether to buy an inclusive package or separate service, whether to buy direct from suppliers, such as airlines or hotels or use an agent , which tour wholesaler or operate or agent to use.

I predict the tourism development in new economic view, it may have these characteristics: Few enterprises in travel and tourism are large, highly cashed-up and have a large asset base, enterprises within travel and tourism that are not in a financial position to diversify, and those do well success to the above –average growth obtainable in travel and tourism compared with many other industries, they would therefore tend to expand within the sector. The result of individual enterprise growth and integration within travel and tourism is an increase in the concentration of that industry. The degree to which output is produced of fewer and fewer enterprises. This can be only be accounted for realistically with the context of an individual economy, Levels of concentration in any part of travel and tourism in the future are likely to depend on two opposing factors: The constant demand by many tourist market segments for new experiences and products, which encourages the development and survival of more and diverse enterprises, and therefore leads to the reduction of concentration as well as technology, which in travel and tourism frequently calls for large capital outlays and requires mass markets for efficient use, promotes integrations and large scale enterprise, especially in air travel and non-personal services (marketing and information communication, travel insurance , tourism payment methods). IN these areas, concentration will undoubtedly increase in future new economic development environment.

● How new economic development in oil industry

The future global economic growth, it will influence personal incomes and GDP rise. They would carry different weight in different countries at different times. Starting from low levels of incomer and economic development. Household consumption will change from being dominated by basic heat to rapidly rising energy use for higher levels of comfort in space heating and cooling (and large dwellings), and greater use of electrical appliances, finally to a degree of saturation influenced by the income distribution patterns of the country concerned. Income distribution typically changes very slowly, so that the technical market for heart will never be saturated because there will always be a proportion of poor people living in small spaces less comfortably than the average. Industrial energy consumption will be influenced by technical efficiency within each sector, and by changes in the structures of the economy, e.g. changing proportions of agriculture, heavy and light industry, and services. One may eventually see evidence of diminishing marginal returns to additional energy inputs compared to other inputs. Energy consumption in the energy transformation sector may be influenced by income, which drives the demand for electricity to influenced by income, which drives the demand for electricity to grow faster than the demand for heat, but is also subject to the chosen technology of transformation, which is influenced by the cost and availability of primary energy inputs (fuels) in new economic development environment.

IN new economic development environment, it will influences that fuels do not compete in all sectors; for example, the transport sector is dominated by oil. Nuclear and hydroelectric power (and most renewables) reach the user through electricity; electricity itself competes with the direct burning of fossil fuels. Electricity provides the means by which other fuels can compete with oil and gas in sectors, such as space heating and process heat. It also is the only means of powering applications such as motors, computers and lighting: these subsectors are difficult to analyze. However, there is strong evidence that higher incomes do not weaken the demand for electricity so much as the demand for energy in total (in contrast to the effect on the demand for non-electric energy forms).

Econometricians look at the historical record of change in fuel prices and quantities to distinguish several factors between the new economic development and old economic development to oil industry in the future. An income effect. Increasing (reducing) fuel prices reduces (increases) the purchasing power of consumers' income: higher incomes caused by lower prices will increase energy consumption; the consumers' allocation of the increased income to energy purchases may reduce as income rises. Thus income may be heading in a different direction from fuel prices that the effect of fuel price changes when incomes are rising means simply that rising incomes have increased demand. Reducing the cost of using energy through win-win efficiency measures causes a similar problem . On the consequence, in future new economic development environment, it may influence in both cases demand will be less than if the future oil price or efficiency has not changed. The other effect is that an efficiency or substitution effect. An increase in fuel prices may cause consumers to spend more on new equipment, building materials and management operations, which will reduce the amount of fuel required to give the same energy result to the user. The extent of the efficiency effect depends on what happens to the price of the new equipment or building: if those price s rise in line with the fuel price, changes in the balances between fuel and capital or management will not occur. A new user technology , such as the development of the combined cycle gas turbine generator may increase efficiency and thus greatly reduce the quantity of primary fuel needed to produce the required output in this case electricity. If electricity prices had remained sticky, and the electricity and gas markets were not competitive, some of this advantages could have accrued to the gas suppliers in the form of an increase in price, because th4 unit of gas produces more output of electricity, it would have a higher value. In reality, the development of new economic competitive environment in both gas and electricity has tended to ensure that the benefits of such technical advanced accrue to the consumer through lower final prices. The same many apply in the case of improved efficiency

in future non-manual driving auto vehicle development: the consumer's cost of motoring is reduced in new economic non-manual driven auto vehicle (Artificial intelligent vehicle) can replace manual driven vehicle , even electricity battery can replace oil energy to be used in vehicles. So, oil price may be influenced to reduce in future new economic development environment.
New and old economic theories explain oil is not main factor
to influence tourism income

● Can economic theory explain old price change to influence tourism income?

I shall attempt to apply old and new economic theory to explain whether oil changing price has direct relationship to influence global tourism indusry development or tourism income as below:

Is oil changing price the main to influence tourism income or tourism development or economic growth ? If oil price rises ar falls, it will or won't cause tourism income decreases or increases? If they have cause and effect relationship, what are the main factors to influence tourism income changes by oil price rises or falls ?

I aim to investigate how any why among oil price shocks will influence tourism income variables. We may distinguish between these oil price shocks: Supply-side , aggregate demand and oil specific demand shocks. I assume that oil specific demand shocks affect inflation and the tourism sector equity index. By constrast, I also believe that aggregate demand oil price shock exercisr an effect, either directly and indirectly tourism generated income and economic growth. So, in old economic theory, supply-side , aggregate demand view to oil specific demand shocks will influence tourism income varies. So, governments ought implement strategies against future oil price movements or plan for economic policy development.

In fact, instead of oil price changes will influence tourism income, it could also harm economic growth and tourism activities, due to the effect they expert on transporation, production cost, economic uncertainty.Because tourism activities is one important sector to influence any country's leisure consumption GDP income source. So, sudden fluctations in oil prices may also influence economic growth. It is based a hyphthesis known as the tourism led economic growth. So, it seems that they have direct or indirect relationship to case effect between oil price and tourism activities and development. So, increase on tourism income, the called " economic-driven tourism growth". In addition, high oil prices are affecting certain tourism industry segments , e.g. airlines, cruises lines, hotel, rent travelling car services etc. for oil, importing countries example, with reference to macro economic effects, higher oil prices generally lead to higher inflation, when they negatively influence to country's income.

Hence, from a micro-economic perspective, positive oil price shocks lead to a decline in disposable income. for low income people, it will bring an immediate and negative impact on tourism, mainly due to they feel tourism leisure is regarded as a luxury good, when oil price shocks to rise suddenly . It influences any airline or cruise entertainment service providers' costs are influenced to raise. Then, they need to increase air ticket or cruise ticket price. It will bring on negative tourism leisure demands-side the oil price increases low income group, potential tourism leisure consumers. Hence, it seems that oil price may have indirect relationship to influence tourism leisure consumers' needs.

● How the price of oil changes influences global tourism industry growth or recession?

In macro-economic view, sudden mid and long term oil price shock can influence global torusim industry growth or recession. For example, a oil price of US$180 per barrel was considered only a few years ago, now this has a realistic scenario to which all plaers in the T&T sector have to adapt. At such a high level, the price of oil will become even more critical to almost every part of the tourism value chain. Although, weak global demand, caused by global economic recesson, resulted in a steep oil price decline to US$45 per barrel by the fourth quarter of 2008 in the past low oil price occurrence history, this won't change the mid to long -term oil forecast.

In fact, the past oil price occurrence history of the dramatic structural had changed a high price imposed on airlines, travelers, and destination countries, all of which will have to navigate through times of shifting or even declining travel demand. I assume that a high oil price scenario is assumed in the long term in order to highlight the changes , such a senario would mean for consumer behavior and the competitiveness of several destinations.

Low oil price in the 1970 and early 1980 did not bring significant growth of international air travel, but its growth has been strongest between 1980 and 2004, a period with stable and relatively moderate oil prices. Also, the rapid development of the low-cost carrier business model in the 1990s further fueled air travel growth by capturing tourism leisure demand , such as weekend leisure travel to cities using mostly secondary airports in any big area countries, such as UK, US . However, the tourism growth is whole influenced by high oil prices, due to oil price had been continue rising in possible.

Basis of oil is shortage supply product, oil is assumed to be the main energy source for the aviation sector for the nest 30 years. Although, second-generation biofuels seem to be on the horizon, the economics as well as the production scalability and aviation biofuel shortage will be a main challenge to airline industry. So, I assume that oil price will continue rise up, if there have none any aviation biofuel can be reflected to oil to use for air plane energy.

Until 2004, the only factors to have affected air travel growth, negatively were in external shocks , such as 9/11, causes catching air plane crisis or US regional geopolitical conflicts. It brings some travelers feel fear to go to US travel, as well as until recently 2019, human mouth disease can influence air to have disease to anyone from mouth. So, global travelers number had been continue decreasing, because they are fear to get disease by air when many themselves every stranger travelers are sitting on the without windows air planes. Although, mouth human and air disease and US 9/11 air attack both matters may influence oil price falls effect, because air planes flying times will reduce. They won't need frequent to fly, to cause aviation oil energy need reduce. Consequently, oil price will decrease, due to travelers number reduces and air planes flying times are also influenced to reduce. (oil demand decreases cause oil price decrease). Although, air lines ' cost will also be influenced reduce, but oil price decrease can not bring travelers number increase , when air ticket price reduce because global many leisure and business trip travelers feel fear to catch air planes frequently when human mouth air disease occured in 2019. So, oil price decreases can not grow up tourism industry growth or rise tourism income.

However, the obvious impact of a high oil price is an increase in the operating costs of airline. Moreover, fuel cost as a percentage of airline operating costs vary significantly based on the length of the flight. The longer the flight, the higher the fuel costs as a percentage of the airline operating cost. So, from an online's perspective, long -hauel flights represent the most criticial challenge to profitable operation because the share of fuel on these flights, compared with other cost items, is largest, because of the unfacorable fuel economics, due to fuel costs even at high-load factors. For example, Thai airways dropped its non-stop Bongkok to US flights in the summer of 2008 for commercial reasons, because fuel reached operating cost levels of 55 percent on this route, a cost burden that could not be passed on to their customers. So, the estimated price elacticity of passengers demand at this Bongkok to US flights route is high, if Thai Airways rises less air ticket price, it will influence many travelers to choose other airlines to catch air plan to fly. Hence, due to Thai Airways can not make decision to rise air ticket price, because it believes that it will lose many travelers, so it only chooses to drop this non-stop Bongkok to US flights to avoid fuel cost rising economic loss.

However, although micro and macro economic theories may also that oil price variable or change, it may influence global tourism income. But, recently, on 2019, human mouth and air diseases, it can influence global individual leisure and business trip travelers feel fear to catch air plans to avoid their bodies get this kind of death sickness when they sit in the no fresh air supplying air planes. They feel that they reduce leisure travelling flying times or business trip flying times with strange travelers to sit in crowd air planes together. Then, they must many avoid human moth and air disease to avoid death crisis. Hence, in this global human mouth and air diseases threat environment occurrence, even oil price sudden reduces to low price, it brings airline's cost reduces and air ticke price reduces. However, when air ticket price reduce to be very cheaper, it can not still attract global many leisure or business trip travelers to buy air tickets to fly frequently. Why does air ticket reduction, it can not attract many leisure or businee trip travelers to buy air ticket to fly ? The main reason is because human mouth and air disease influences global many travelers feel fear to catch air planes frequently. In psychological view, this kind of human mouth and air sickness will bring long time negative influence to global traveles do not want to catch air planes for business trips or travelling leisure frequently. So, it implies that oil price changing to influence air ticket price reduction factor ought not main factor to influence tourism income. It may include traveler individual negative emotion psychological factor, such as human mouth and air disease or 2019 9/11 attack both cases, they can influence global travelers feel fear to catch air planes to fly to avoid death threat. So, oil changing price ought not be only one absolute main factor to influence global tourism income significantly.

On conclusion, in economic view, it seems that oil chang price may have indirect or direct relationship to influence tourism income, instead of some unpredicted external environment factors influence, such as US 9/11 attack crisis and human mouth and air disease factors, they may be main factors to influence travellers number to reduce in non-economic external unpredicted environment view.

CHAPTER FIVE

International war and illness factors influences tourism industry development

1.1 Can wars impact global tourism threat?

1.1.1 How did First World War influence Europe economy and tourism industry declines ?

Can wars bring either advantages or disadvantages or both to impact our economy growth ?In history, I feel that international war can influence any country's economy development has either positive or negative impact in possible.

On the inflationary hand, for the First World War economy growth influence example, in the First World War and since most notably the German hyperinflation of the 1920 year, this type of monetary regime shows a far smaller tendency towards inflation. In the First World War period, volatility of inflation and output were higher in the short run. So, First World War had little negative impact to influence world inflation in the war period. However, in the First World War period, the supply of money was determined not by the rates of economic growth only, but by the amount of available gold and could not be adjusted in response to economic needs. So, new sources of gold would increase money supply and inflation and decrease interest rates , the opposite of what modern central banks would do to provide stable economic growth in First World War. So, it explained that the First World War occurrence caused the change from non-inflationary to inflationary long term development. Thus, it seems First World War brings more money supply and gold supply to stable economic growth in the future long term period.

On the labor productivity influence hand, leaving monetary issues aside, the First World War created the working time intellectual mood to change labor productivity, it would be a 15-18 hours working week for more enlightened leisure to Europe labors. Some prominent modern economists on the accuracy of the predictions on GDP growth per capital was remarkably accurate given to be fallen down that it was made at the time when economy growth theory did not even exist in the First World War period. Thus, it seems First World War also causes working time to be raised to the developing countries during the industrialization period. Then, the long time working time brought to the developing countries' workers to it is poor for labor health. Hence, although employers can raise productivity, but they need many workers to work long time to cause unhealthy. The majority found that the prediction on leisure is of the variations between world regions , due to income level exist, making European variety of capitalism. So, the First World War caused income inequality within countries and between nation states, trends in working hours , world poverty and ever growing needs (consumerism) and the like. Thus, the developed western countries' workers can work lesser time to compare to the developing Asia countries' workers. Consequently, First World War brought negative impact to influence the developing Asia countries' worker unhealthy and physical and mental illnesses number had been increasing as well as it brought positive impact to influence the labor productivity had been increasing to the Asia countries' employers, due to their workers need to work long time every day.

It seems on the positive impact hand, that the First World War caused the inflation occurrence to bring more money supply and gold supply to be raised to influence global economic growth. But, on the negative impact hand, it also brought low working hours in European developed countries and high working hours to the Asia developing countries which are needed to do different occupations in developing countries as well as the income inequality caused unfair social challenge had also occurred in developed countries, such as Europe, UK, US etc. and developing countries, such as China, Japan, Korea etc . Thus, First World War had brought developed countries better economy development and better salary and less working hours to labors because Europe had reached the mature stage of industrialization to avoid labors who needed to work overtime. Otherwise, it had brought developing countries poor economy development and poor salary and labors need work long time to raise productivities.

In conclusion, it implied that the First World War had bought some bad influences to developing countries' economic system, e.g. social income inequality, working hours inequality, inflation and GDP per capita going down in the past Europe economic history development, but it also bought welfares to developed countries' European labor working time intellectual mood to change labor productivity, it would be a 15-18 hours working week for more enlightened leisure to Europe labors. So, it seemed to cause negative economic influence to developing countries, but it cause positive economic influence to developed counties during the First World War time.

● Can US poor economic consequences of war influence tourism industry growth?

What are the macroeconomic effects of US government spending on the war? I believe modern times are that the human cost military spending has created positive economic outcomes for the US economy. I shall indicate how the human costs of war influences positive economic outcomes for the US on these aspects which include: GDP, consumption , investment , inflation and income distribution aspects.

In fact, US heightened military spending can create employment additional economic activity and contributes to the military weapon development of new technologies, which can bring advantages into other industries in US. For long term economic influence, US military weapon research and development on creating employment would potentially have the same low cost economic benefit in US. For example, US economy had higher GDP growth in the Afghanistan and Iraq war period. Another benefit is that US had appropriate conditions for future growth after the Second World War great depression period. It was a sharp decline in income inequality and the trend in declining inequality standard after the Second World War great depression period. Thus, America's human cost military spending could bring indirect military weapon research and development on creating employment benefit and it would potentially have the same low cost economic benefit in US. However, in the war period, the higher levels of government military weapon spending with war tends to generate some positive economic benefits in the short-term period, specifically through increases in economic growth during spending booms after war period.

Why it can bring GDP growth in the US war period. In general, by the end of World Ward II, US GDP was over 120 % and tax revenue increased more than three times to over 20% of GDP. However, GDP growth there was are increase in the trend lines after the war had finished when unemployment was eliminated, recovery was well underway prior to the war, are the key counterfactual is whether similar spending on US public works would have generated even more growth. However, US macroeconomic history over the past seventy years, that there are a number of negative economic effects from conducting any wars. But, there have also positive benefits of increases US government tent spending on military industry. Moreover, when an economy has excess capacity and unemployment , it is possible that increasing military spending can provide an important stimulus. When military and defense spending is important in providing security for the US nation as well as helping to support and protect US's national affect.

So, in war economic view point, it will bring this question: Is efficiency or justification for any particular macroeconomic effects of war spending for US? To answer this question, I shall suppose security is not only dependent on an adequate military capability , but security can also keep on economic stability. For example, price controls strategy and rationing strategy had a significant role to play to influence consumption in US, during war period. For example, it was difficult for household to purchase products , such as washing machines, irons or water heaters because the raw resources, e.g. steel and production capabilities are needed to be used to produce military weapons instead of these products effort to prepare to fight the enemy in the Second World War. So, the raw resources, e.g. steel price will be rasied, due to shortage to supply to produce the home consumer products , Then, it will bring the home consumer products price to be raised. So, war will bring negative impact to influence home consumer product prices to be raised, due to shortage of steel resources supply when they are supplied to produce weapon to win enemy in war period. Consequently, In war period negative resource shortge hand, as the same time, the war production board was able to assign priorities to scare materials, such as rubber, steel and aluminum to ensure which went to production of the military, rather than to civilian products. In addition, wages were controlled and personal savings were encouraged through the purchase of war bonds which further limited the size of individual's disposable income during the Second World War period.

Moreover, in the war period, it also bring food price raising, due to food supply shortage and poor living standrd to poor people, even rich people. Due to people were also encouraged to conserve food and produce as much of that own food as possible because food items were generally scare. Freezes were also stayed for wages. Combined with a general reduction in consumption, it can be said living standards for whose already employed, at least in material terms did not improved , even to rich people. It means that war will influence people quality of life to be fallen down. Even, in terms of total GDP. Such as World War II (WWII) did not create a permanent increase or change in the growth the trend after the war had ended. However, the positive lasting effort for WWII was a more even distribution of wealth. This reallocation of income created the ideal conditions for the formation of an advancement consumer economy till to nowadays.

However, on war long time influence hand, the WWII influenced US economy to be changed to be better, such as material well being was affected by tax increases, new price and wage controls which constrained private sector consumption and investment is encouraged, due to World War II had destroyed the traditional material development, so it also encouraged new investors to invest to any Asia or Europea new businesses.

● Can war economy policy influence peace and security?

I believe war economics policy may contribute to international peace and security as positive impact more than negative impact. The reasons are as below:

A first positive attitude behavioral possibility , any war economic policy can increase international interdependence through trade and finance raises the potential costs of war to a degree that makes welfare an irrational option of foreign policy can raise economic growth and builds good trading relationship between countries. Moreover, the use of superior economic and military power to harm an actual or potential aggressor's economy and make it stops preparing of waging war, e.g. US restricted Mexico imported to itself country, US invented military weapons to threaten to Korea to avoid nuclear war occurrence. In the past, US spent to military expenditure which could rise to employ soldier numbers to reduce unemployment as well as assisted military weapon manufacturers needed to employ many manufacturing workers to manufacture many military weapons for US government military fighting need.

Hence, the relationship between war and economy will bring this basic question: Whether either can economics provide a growing tool for avoiding war or whether may consumption for resources and markets result in an increased likelihood of war? Following the increase of international trade and financial transfers in modern times. However, there has been a growing to concern the economic wisdom of war.

Liberal economists oppose the idea that war might be a good business and advocated the promotion of peace and advocated the promotion of peace by international economic links among the different countries. Although, history has shown that enlightened economic self-interest was not always alike to contribute to the ultimate avoidance of war. But, a short overview of the liberal peace theory indicates, it takes a look at the amount ability of economic instruments as a means to enforce peace by an economically superior country or group of countries, e.g. within the framework of the United Nations or of regional organization for security and cooperation in Europe, the African Union or the organization of American States.

1.1.4 How civil wars influence positive or negative impact to traveler leisure needs?

On country itself civil war negative impact hand, what is the impact of civil wars on economic growth at domestic and in nearby countries? Some economists believe civil war can have a profound negative influence on the economic fortunes of a country or its neighbors, e.g. owing to a loss of human capital, a destruction of infrastructure and reductions in investment and trade and daily market activities. Within the period of measurement have economic consequences , the economists scale the civil war variable to be better identify their relative impacts. They indicate the distance between countries which is a factor provides the most accurate measure of the negative economic consequences of civil wars on other countries.

On country itself civil war positive impact hand, in economic view point, the country itself civil war indicates the income and capital input terms. Since, everything is in per capita terms. Due to civil war encourage technological development. Technology changes are in the investment in labor effectiveness. The capital includes physical and human capital . How civil war influences efficiency growth . The growth in labor's enhanced efficiency is from technology change and capital depreciation. So, anything that can raise labor growth or its improved efficiency, increases the denominator or capital per capita and so reduced its growth and that of incomer per capita. Depreciation or the gradual wearing down of capita; through use or age also limits capital growth. Some economists suggest that war migration is a good growth of labor to influence the immigration country's economic growth. For example, the inflow of refugees from a nearby civil war can lead to in-migration and adversely affect income per capita growth. Migration may , however, influences the in-migration country economic growth if the migrants bring in human capital, due to civil war.

Consequently, from a theoretical perspective, civil wars can adversely affect income per capita growth at home through a number of avenues. So civil war will cause bad influence to home country, the reasons are as below:

The reasons include:

First, a civil conflict can destroy physical and human capital. Second, by the international trade flows, and day-to-day marketing activities, civil wars can inhibit growth. Third, civil wars may divert the inflow of foreign direct investment (FDI) owing to heightened perceived risks of investors. Because (FDI) perceived is an imported source of savings that finances investment. So, a fill in FDI results in reduced growth. Heightened instability and risks will also limit investment at home and cause a flight of savings abroad. Fourth, civil wars cause indirect government defense expenditures from productive social overhead capital e.g. roads, public schools and bridges, gardens to less productive defense spending. Fifth, such wars may cause the internal displacement of people as their homes either come under serious control or are destroyed. So that income per capita is adversely influenced. Sixth, civil wars often result in the breakdown of the health lead to lack of medical care, less clean drinking water and reduced sanitation , all of which have negative consequences on economic activities and growth .

Thus, any country itelf civil war can bring negative impacts more than positive impacts. Due to economic impacts may even increase further from some conflicts as nearby countries reduce trade with others in the regions and potential investors brand , even non-neighboring countries have as poor investment risks. Thus, there are four potential channels , such as human capital, physical capital, labor growth and an intercept shift are influenced by civil wars as well as which can influence income per capita growth in other nearby countries. To conclude, neighboring countries need to concern how to avoid civil war is caused to occur among themselves because civil wars will have negative impact to influence their economic growth.

● How economic positive and negative impact of the war to higher military spending?

Most models show that military spending to divert resources from productive uses, such as consumption and investment , and ultimately slows economic growth and reduces employment. So, it seems war causes disadvantages more than advantages to influence economy growth to any countries in possible.

Some economists showed global insight produced a set of projections that compared a scenario with an increase in annual military spending equal to 1.0% of GDP current about $135billions relative to its baseline scenario . This is approximately equal to the increase in defense spending that has taken place compared with the pre-Sept. 11th terrorism Iraq war baseline to US government higher military spending. However, who also indicated military spending is not generally perceived to cost jobs.

In standard economic models, war its positive impact can be thought of in the same way as spending on the environment from war bad influence. When tax and emission restrictions are often used to achieve environment protection during and after war. It is also possible to reach environmental targets by paying people to do things that will reduce pollution. For example, it is possible to reduce greenhouse gas emissions by paying people to buy more fuel efficient cars and appliances, or paying than to install insulation and other energy saving devices. So, during the war period, more greenhouse gas fuel efficient cars will increase demand in car market. Thus, war can reduce air and water pollution cost and encourage greenhouse gas fuel consumption. In the case of both increased military spending and paying people to take steps to reduce greenhouse gas emissions, resources would be reduced to supply to these countries' domestic market directed uses.

In standard economic models, war it's negative impact to this redirection of other resources, due to the original resources are used to increase military spending to manufacturing any new weapons and it will cause this original resources are shortage to prepare for these countries' manufacturing countries. So, these resources shortage challenges will cause these military spending countries' economy to operate less efficiently and therefore lead to slower growth and fewer jobs supplies. Thus, war will bring resource shortage challenges and fewer jobs supplies bad influence. In policy debates, it is important to recognize the potential jobs losses are caused from military spending factor mainly. Also the potential economic costs are often a factor in debates over environment policy.

Due to war causes the military countries' air and water pollution challenges. So, the military countries' wars occurrence will raise the water and air pollution cost of chance. It is often believed environmental pollution challenge has relationship between wars and increases in military spending. So, in this way, any country is carrying on military spending is comparable in most models to any other form of any country's spending, such as spending on public products or improving the environment pollution expenditures. Thus, it seems war will bring environment pollution economic cost more than environment protection economic benefit to any military expending countries.

Country itself internal civil war influences

2.1 The relationship between country itself internal civil war and human welfare

2.1.1 How internal civil war influences human welfare?

Nowadays, a growing number of economists and political scientists often ask this simple question: Why there is so much civil wars in any country itself the world? Poverty is commonly held to be a leading cause of internal wars. Indeed, it has close relationship between low per capita incomes and higher propensities for internal war's countries. Such as developing country Africa, it has many times more internal wars. So, it brings poverty and low living standards and poor health and poor air and water pollution environment to let African to live. Then, hunger and disease will also be caused easily in Africa.

However, internal civil wars also bring negative influences to developed countries, such as Australia, US Canada, UK , Japan, Korea etc. countries. The reason is because the internal civil war counties which refugee flows will choose to immigrate to those developed countries. Such as developing countries, South Korea and Africa and India , there have many times more internal civil wars .So it brings poverty and low living standards and poor health and poor environment to let African , South Korean, Indian to choose to live to these developed countries. Then, hunger and disease will be caused easily in developing and developed both countries, due to developed countries permit these developing countries' refugee who immigrate to themselves countries to live from internal civil war counties refugee immigration easily.

Moreover, internal civil war can also influence developed countries, such as Australia, US, Canada , UK refugee flows will choose to immigrate to these developed countries lawlessness as well as the illicit trades in drugs , arms and minerals will appear into these developed countries neighboring conflict zones . The destructive consequences of internal civil welfare may be a great as to potentially be a factor in the growing gap between the world's richest and poorest nations.

2.1.2 Can internal civil wars influence the country's long run economic development to assist tourism industry experience growth cycle stage?

Has it relationship between long run economic growth and internal civil war? Some economists recommend that it focuses on impacts on capital and population, the basic of economic production and whether the internal civil war country is possible rapid recovery as well as the internal civil wars cause economic impacts which can also been found for human capital, including measures of education, nutrition, health and productivity to the internal civil war countries.

What are intenal civil war negative impacts? Some behavior economists had experimented one interesting research to indicate that any internal civil war country will reduce human resource productivity growth , will reduce overall GDP in possible. Their research indicated the internal war armed group leaders are most motivate citizens to be soldiers for their side. Participation becomes easier to motivate the lower is citizen's opportunity cost of fighting . So there models predict that the amount of citizens' time devoted to fighting increases as the returns to fighting rise relative to the returns to reduce human resources supply to society to assist enterprises to raise any productive activities.

Consequently, in economic view point, if the internal civil war countries citizen will be trained to be soldiers. Then, it will reduce citizen to do other occupations in the internal war period. Also, the internal civil war countries will reduce their citizen have time and effort to do other social occupations to assist countries' economy development in the internal civil war period. Moreover, the internal civil war countries citizen, such as human resource number will be shortage to supply to satisfy their countries' enterprises' needs in the internal civil war period. It will influence economic growth to be go down during the internal civil war period to the internal civil war countries for either short term or long term. Even, the natural resource supply, e.g. water, food, vehicle gas etc. will be concentrate on spending to satisfy the soldiers' needs. It will cause natural resource shortage to supply to satisfy to citizen's life needs daily in the natural civil war period. So, the internal civil war will bring disadvantage to influence economic growth to the internal civil war countries.

2.1.3 How can reduce the risks of the civil internal war to influence economy growth and cause traveler individual tourism need reduces?

How can reduce the risks when internal civil war occurs in the country? What factors explain variations in the duration of civil internal wars, and why should policymakers care? I shall suppose to the duration of civil internal wars , which should be implicated in their destructiveness to the civil internal war country as well as long time duration of civil internal wars should have long time poor economic influence to the civil internal war country.

At any given point in a civil internal war, the civil internal war country government (A) and the civil internal war country rebels(B) each must choose between stopping or continuing to flight.

This implies four possible outcomes from their joint decisions at any time.

The first outcome is that if (B) continues flight and (A) stops, (B) wins and the government (A) is overthrown.

The second outcome is that if government (A) flights and (B) stops, (A) wins and the revolt is defeated (B) .

The third outcome is that if both (A) and (B) choose to stop flight at the same time, the civil internal war ends to be a negotiated settlement.

The fourth outcome is that if neither decides to stop, the civil internal war continues (Stam 1996 , 34-37).

Stam (1996, 353) again indicated the four outcomes can be represented as an two person game. Continued flight is the dominant strategy for both sides.

Thus, it seems negotiated settlement is the best solution to solve any civil internal war because it won't have either win or loss outcome to either of party, it will have win outcome to both countries.

In economic welfare view point, they will discuss how to earn the much economic benefits to achieve the reasonable negotiation fairly. It is a two parties win-to-win method to both supported government and not supported government parties both. Because usually the cause of any internal civil war , due to the not supported (disagreed) government party feel whose government is unfair to give reasonable and fair much economic welfare to them in society. So, they (part of citizen) only choose to cause internal civil war to let their country to know that who feel dissatisfactory at the time.

In economic view point, unfair resource allocation challenge will cause any internal civil war easily in any country. Thus, it means that any country government ought to know when and how to allocate its limited resources to let its citizen to feel fair to use (spend) in society when resources are not shortage to supply to them to consume. Also, it means how to allocate (spend) limited resource to prepare any countries' citizen to enjoy to consume. So, it is one important question to any country government to concern if which wanted to reduce internal civil war occurrence chance on nowadays societies. Thus, it seems that any country itself internal civil war will bring disadvantages more than advantages to bring its tourism leisure industy experiences declines cycle stage easily in possible

Bibliography

Stam , A. C. 1996, Win, Lose or Draw: Domestic politics and the crucible of war . Ann Arbor: University of Michigan Press.

Economic recession or boom how influences consumer behavior when the business had been experiencing decline life cycle stage
● COVID -19 disease how influence businesses may experience either growing life cycle stage or decline life cycle stage.
Nowadays, we are facing global economic recession period, since COVID 19 human mouth disease effect can bring economic crisis. Can it influence businesses feel difficult to adapt how global economic recession change after their decline life cycle stage? However, the effects of COVID 19 spreading will have wider implication , not just on how economies function, but also on how consumers behave, across china, Asia-pacific and around the world. Another effect of China;s economic rise is its influence in the adoption and adaption to new technological invention to manufacture , e.g. manufacturing robotic products had sold to China factories to replace workers to manufacturer products. It also will influence many China manufacturing workers lose jobs, when many China factories apply manufacture robotics to replace them in nowadays economic recession period.
Considering the adoption of online-offline shopping and home online office tasks, they are influenced by COVID-19 human disease influence, it also influences on regional travel in China, even global travel income is also reducing, because many travelers feel afraid to catch air planes to avoid to get COVID 19 human disease when they are sitting in close window airplanes by air . HOwever, COVID 19 also influences global consumer behavior changes to online shopping, because many people are afraid to enter crowd shops to avoid get COVID 19 human disease easily. So global shops will lose many visiting shop consumers, if they do not decide to attempt to open online stores to let customers to apply internet to buy their products. So, COVID 19 human mouth disease induced changes in consumer behavior. Shop online will be one new trend to influence young and old consumers make shopping from online stores. They will enquire whether the kind of product is worth to choose to buy by social media, e.g. facebook,

online post . Hence, COVID19 human mouth disease may influence global economic recession, but it also brings e-commerce boom chance, when many consumers are fear to enter any crowd shops , when they need to stay long time in any shops. Then, they get COVID 19 human mouth disease chance will increase. Hence, it will influence many customers reduce to visit shops times, but it also creates online-shopping new business model . For example, China families are renewing their joy in home cooking. Onlins cooking videos are helping with the discovery od new recipes, new ways to create dishes , and new influences. So, opportunities are opening for more cleaning products, new ways to clean and new home hacks from online videos will bring global home consumers spend more time on their wellness or beauty routines ? So, COVID-19 disease also influences many families choose to cook dinner at homes at nght. Restaurants will lose many eating clients, because they are fear to enter restaurants to eat together to avoid to get COVID19 human mouth disease. But, it also creates home cooking products sale chance, e.g. rice cookers, dishes or any cooking tools because many families choose to cool at home. Hence, in some situation, economic recession will create new business chance , such as online store or rice cooker sale increases, they may be influenced in this COVID 19 human mouth disease occurrence environment.

Economic recession also influences business strategy changes. Many companies seem to be applying many aspects of a retrenchment approach , e.g. reduced fixed costs, narrower product offering, reduced staffs, but also there are some aspects of an investment approach which can be observed , because customers number will be influenced to reduce in economic recession environment. Companies have felt the robustness and quality of the approaches being applied had been allowed to decline. As a consequence of the challenges of a recession, urgent improvement have needed to be made because factories will reduce workers number to avoid salary expenditure spending more , but customers umber reduced in recession environment .

Hence, they will choose to buy manufacturing robotics to replace workers. If robotics can be improved to be proficient manufacture. Then, they won't need to buy many robotics to help them to replace to replace many workers to manufacture any products efficiently. So, manufacturing and improvement to robotics number demand may increase to any factories , e.g. vehicle manufacture, electronic products, e.g. computer hime cooking electronic products , e.g. rice cookers, heaters etc. products may be manufactured by manufacturing robotics. It creates the manufacturing robotic sale improvement quality chance in recession environment. It may impact on medium, or long term, it depends on how long time of recession. So, economic recession may bring robotic manufacture industry boom , when electronic products manufacturers need many improved robotics to replace workers in factries in order to reduce spending too much salaries expenditure in recession.

It is one external environmental factor to influence sudden manufacture robotic industry boom absolutely ,because electronic manufacturer's manufacturing robotic needs increases in recession environment. So, robotic manufacturers' strategy need to change , such as how to improve any manufacturers' needs in recession, e.g. manufacturing robotic product categories, market segments, geographic areas, core technologies, reliability , price, customisation, robotic manufacturing efficiency how to be improved of business.Change strategy to any manufacturing robotics manufacturers. So, recession may influence some kinds of manufacturing robotics' needs raise in robotic manufacturing market.

● How recession influences the role of advertising changes?

Advertising plays a key role in a dynamic economy. It may provide valuable information about products and services in an efficient manner, communicates client value, builds brand awareness and creates demand. However, when one country is experiencing recession, how it influences the country's businessmen spending on advertisement behaviors? Due to clients number reduces, a company usualy cuts come from the advertising budget than companies begin to cut back on advertiseing during an economic recession, they become less visible to the public because they predict clients number ought reduce next three months, even half year or one year. It depends on how long economt recession occurs. So, economic recession many impact any companies' advertising budget expenditure to be reduce . How much on the reduction on advertising budget expenditure, it depends on the company predicts how many clients number will reduce.However, due to advertising number reduces, it can influence consumer behavior changes indirectly.

In economic boom environment, consumers can watch to different kinds advertisement from television. Advertisement may bring positive alternative evaluation phase of biying decision-making process is bring exposed to buy several communication messages. In such an economic boom environment, any organizations may be clearly heard by the consumers, after any advertisement programs are broadcasted on television. Therefore, advertisemtn can persuade clients to choose to buy the kind of product after the kind of product advertisement is broadcasted from television absolutely. However, when recession occurs, any companies; advertisement time is shortened , even number is reduced . Hence, they can not receive any client's positive or negative feedback immediately in short time afer advertisements are broadcasted from television . So, recession may influence advertisement time is shortened and number is rediced . On consequence, companies can not have any repsonse to know whether how market or customers' demand is changing to themselves products in shor time.

However, recession may bring worse advertisement effect to influence any businesses . On one hand, there is a negative economic recession environment because of the negative media reporting, these would be a decline in demand for the products and services and eventually companies would want to save more than they spend , But in the other hand, when the companies cut back advertiseing expenditures, they become less visible to public. Hence recession may influence many companies brand image will be lost, due to spending on advertisement expenditure wil reduce.

Then, clients number may be influenced to reduce, because they can not watch the kind of product advertisment from television home often.

When one country is encountering recession, how are the various components of household consumption affected ? How is the impact of the recesion distributed across socio-demographic group? How does the recession compare to previous recessions? When book will boom? In fact, any country's recession may impact consumer behavior changes, it depends on these factors: age, race, education and wealth groups resulted in a decline in consumption inequality. The rich group is the " wealth effect influence group" when recession comes, it may influence their wealth reduces, so their enjoyment dsires will be influenced to reduce, e.g. purchase expensive cars driving enjoyment desires, purchase expensive house living enjoyment desires. If one rich person loses jobs , it may influence him to spend less time to drive themselves cars, so consumption of gasline will be influenced to reduce.

Economic theory (e.g. consumer behavioral economic theory) predicts that when economic recession occurs, it will cause many businesses may experience decline cycle life stage rapidly, that link between income shocks and consumption has close relationship, such as rich person consumer group, if his income reduces, then he will buy less gas to drive himself car, even if he loses his job in recession environment, he will choose to sell his car to exchange cash. Hence, consumption may fall as a direct consequence of a fall in income induced by job loss, reduced hours or productivity and negative returns from assets, if there are long term changes to a household's econmic resource in recession environment. Hence, in recession environment, job loss or income reduction factors that may affect consumers and their shopping attitudes in the recession period. Otherwise, for low income group, recession may influence food consumption to low income consumer behavior changes to worse. Because low income person may reduce income ot lose job, then cheap food consumption will be influenced to worse to low income consumer group.

In recession period, if the food price is raised , due to the cost increase of food, it will lead to change in the reductin on quantity and type of food being purchase to low income food buyers. This may lead to a reduction in the quantity of food consumed and/ or the substitution of high-priced food for cheaper food, which is often less nutritous and of worse quality. Hence in recession perios, low income food consumers will consider whether the kind of food price has how much increase or decrease. They won't consider the quantity of food consumed for maintaining energy balance and the quality of food consumed for maintaining ample intakes of protains, fats and micronutrients, such as vitamins, minerals and trace elements on food issue. So, if the kind of food price reduced in recession period, it ought may attract many low income food consumers number, even its food nutritious is worse. Hence, if the kind of meat price can be reduced in recession , the cheap types of meat consumption to low income consumer may be increased, even its nutritious is worse to compare the recession occurs before period.

On conclusion, in either economic recession or boom period, in general, consumer behavior will be influenced to change. Some products may be influenced to have higher sale in recession period, e.g. home electronic rice cookers , due to COVID 19 human mouth disease influenced many households choose to cook dinner at home at ight. Otherwise, some products may be influenced to have lowr sale., e.g. expensive cars sale in recession period, many high income people may lose jobs or reduce salaries , then it will influence their car purchase desires to be reduced. But if COVID 19 human mouth disease has medicine to kill this kind of disease. Then, economy will boom, many households will choose to go to restaurants to eat dinner. The, the electronic rice cookers sale number may reduce, when they reduce time to cook at home at night. Hence, it explains why economic recession or boom period may have impact to influence consumer behavior in behavioral economic view.

Illness influences tourism leisure need

Our global tourism development had been developed from birth cycle stage to decline life cycle stage nowadays. From 1960 beginning, when airplanes were popular to be increased need to global travelers. Hence, from 1960 to 1970 is whole global tourism industry birth cycle stage. Till to 1971 beginning, many Asia, e.g. Singapore, Japan, China and Western, e.g. UK, UK etc. countries people, they have jobs to do ,and they have more extra money to prepare to choose any leisure activities. From 1971 to 1980, it is growth life cycle stage to global tourism industry. Many airplane manufacturers had been beginning to manufacturer many airplanes because they felt global traveler number would increase. In fact, in this ten years, global traveler number had been increasing every year. Then, from 1981 to 2019 this fourty years, it is global tourism industry nature life cycle stage. It means that every year travel number had been increasing more significantly to compare past. Also, many travelers feel need to travel every year. So, global travel tourism industry may reach the most top travel clients level in this fourty years. However, till to 2020 , due to COVD19 human mouth and disease occurrence, it influences global travelers feel fear to catch air planes to travel because this kind COVD 19 human mouth disease may cause lung disease from air. When many travelers are sitting in the close window air plane, if one person has ths kind COVD19 human mouth disease. The sick person may contact air to let the persons to breath to cause lung disease in possible in airplane. So, global travelers number is decreasing after 2019 . Also, it implies that tourism industry is facing decline life cysle stage.

It brings these questions: IS it right time to develop space tourism? Can space tourism help future tourism industry to re-grow its life cycle stage from nowadays decline life cycle stage? Can space tourism develop to nature stage from birth life cycle stage ? I shall attempt to give evidence to explain whether space tourism may be developed to let human has more one kind tourism . It may be future leisure new trend for travelers, instead of earth travel. Because one day earth tourism destination may not bring leisure interesting to global traveler, then space tourism may be attempted to replace this kind of travelling activity . So, space tourism is birth life cycle stage. However, our earth tourism may define moral tourism, nature tourism, green tourism, responsible tourism in future new travelling leisure trend.

It bring these questions: Can our future tourism industry meet the expectations with the terms " ecological tourist"? Which factors affect the product life cycle of eco tourism? Nature and green tourism may be our earth new kind of travel activities, when many young and old age travelers like to climb mountains, they feel life nature scene more than non-man made) nature scene in their journeys, they do not like to visit cities to travel. It is possible that they often work in offices, this office working factor may influence many travelers like green tourism in the future. So, green or nature tourism will be our future popular tourism leisure activities. It may influence nowadays our tourism decline life stage to re-grown to nature life cycle stage in possible in this COVD19 people mouth disease influential environment.

New economic development in Tourism and oil industries

● How to develop new economic tourism industry

How to develop tourism industry in new economic environment? Any examination of the new economic development of travel and tourism requires definitions of the subject and its components, which are suitable for economic analysis. However, in new economic development to tourism industry, it is also important to look at tourism conceptually, in order to set the scene for a deeper understanding of the future new tourism industry development.

Tourism is neither a phenomenon nor a simple set if industries, however, in new or old economic development environment. It is a human activity which encompasses human behavior, use of resources, and interaction with other people, economies and leisure enjoyment environment. It is also involved physical movement of tourists to locales other than their normal living places.

In future new economic environment, traditional travel needs to include these element in order to satisfy traveler enjoyment and leisure feeling: They may include: Tourist needs and motivations, tourism selection and behavior and constraints , travel away from home , market interactions between tourists and those supplying products to satisfy tourist needs and impacts on tourists , hosts, economies and environments.

In new economic environment, the tourism products may include: carriers, in any forms of transport for tourist travel accommodation, man-made attractions, which could also include the managed areas of natural attractions, private sector and public sector support services, middlemen, such as tour wholesalers and travel agents.

The tourism resources may also include: Natural resources, lands , minerals, water and biological; labor resources, human work, and enterprise; capital resources, manmade enhancement and other resources. The travel and tourism resources problems may include: As there is frequently a mismatch between producer and consumer perception of what constitutes the tourism product , there may be conflict in ideas of which resources are properly involved as well as many of the resources likely to be in demand for tourism are public goods , or even free resources.

In new economic development to tourism industry view, we need to consider that tourism and travel has the reputation of being a relatively clean and pleasant industry in which to work or invest in order to attract a greater number of resource suppliers than as less well-perceived industry, which therefore keeps rewards prices down by competition, how to attract those retiring from or travel business for example, if their finances are already sound, income from travel is not expected to be optimal , travel and tourism is frequently highly seasonal , offering rewards that are competitive with other industries only some of the time, destination products are often in locations which are of little use to other industries, so that competition for resource use if minimal and hence rewards are low.

In general, tourist purpose may include: recreational purpose : holiday, health and sport and religion as well as business purpose: company business , e.g. conventions and sales trips. So, in new economic tourism development aim, tourism industry need consider hoe to achieve incentive trips to let these both tourists to feel. For example, the overall type of tourism required, destination arrangement, travel mode, accommodation and attraction visiting and purchasing method or distribution channel. The purchasing method choices may include: whether to buy an inclusive package or separate service, whether to buy direct from suppliers, such as airlines or hotels or use an agent , which tour wholesaler or operate or agent to use.

I predict the tourism development in new economic view, it may have these characteristics: Few enterprises in travel and tourism are large, highly cashed-up and have a large asset base, enterprises within travel and tourism that are not in a financial position to diversify, and those do well success to the above –average growth obtainable in travel and tourism compared with many other industries, they would therefore tend to expand within the sector. The result of individual enterprise growth and integration within travel and tourism is an increase in the concentration of that industry. The degree to which output is produced of fewer and fewer enterprises. This can be only be accounted for realistically with the context of an individual economy, Levels of concentration in any part of travel and tourism in the future are likely to depend on two opposing factors: The constant demand by many tourist market segments for new experiences and products, which encourages the development and survival of more and diverse enterprises, and therefore leads to the reduction of concentration as well as technology, which in travel and tourism frequently calls for large capital outlays and requires mass markets for efficient use, promotes integrations and large scale enterprise, especially in air travel and non-personal services (marketing and information communication, travel insurance , tourism payment methods). IN these areas, concentration will undoubtedly increase in future new economic development environment.

HOW TO PROLONG TOURISM LEISURE MATURE LIFE CYCLE STAGE AS WELL AS AVOID DECLINE AND DEATH LIFE

CYCLE STAGE OCCURENCE FROM COVID 19 HUMAN DISEASE
Any businesses expect to reach the mature life service cycle stage and they also hope to prolong to stay in this stage and avoid to have chance experience decline life service cycle stage, even death stage in future whole business life cycle stages. However, in fact, there are many businesses need to spend long time to have effort to reach mature life cycle stage from birth and growth both stages, even when they have effort to experience this the topest level stage, many can not stay to prolong time in this stage, then they will reach next stage, such as decline life cycle stage, even final death life cycle stage possibly. Hence , research whether how can reach the mature life cycle stage in short time and prolong to say in this stage. It is one common researching value question to any businesses. Such as COVID 19 human disease had been occurrence in 2019 end , it bring global tourism industry traveller number began to reduce. I shall attempt to explain how airline organizations implement strategies to avoid to enter decline service life cycle stage as below:

● How to avoid to reach the decline service life stage rapidly to global airlines tourism service industry due to COVID 19 human disease occurred

Strategies for growing and maturity a product or raise service performance, and increasing profit margins and prolonging to stay on the mature service life stage. I believe that it is any service businesses final aim. However, in any service life cycle stages, when the service , e.g. airline tourism leisure service industry will experience the decline service life stage , due to the COVID19 human disease influences to global travelers began to feel fear to catch airplanes to avoid air contact to give this kind of disease from 2020. So, nowadays, airlines ought have the suitable or right strategies to help them to solve travelers reducing number to influence their profit growth to encounter decline life service cycle stage later.

Life cycle strategy is based on product or service life cycle thinking from marketing, the factors may influence when the business can reach the mature life cycle stage, but some unpredicted factors may influence their clients number reduce, such as this airlines organizations traveler number reduces is due to COVID 19 human disease influences they feel fear to catch airplanes to travel case, their strategies may include: market growth rate, market growth potential, breach of service lines, number of competitor, distribution of market, share among competitors, customer loyalty , barriers to entry and technology improvement etc. factors to influence the global airlines tourism service industry can continue develop or expand to future overseas tourism market, when COVID 19 human disease may be killed by new medicine later.

Such as this COVID 19 human disease influences travelers feel fear to catch airplanes to avoid get this kind of disease and it influences global travelers number is decreasing in 2020 case, when the airline organization reaches the growth life service cycle stage from the birth stage, if it expects to spend short time to reach the mature life service cycle stage. Before COVID 19 human disease had not been killed by new medicine, if they hope to attract many travelers to choose to catch their airplanes to fly , the extension strategies that any airline organization can attempt to achieve, they may include, rebranding, establishing airline service in order to differentiate the other airline competitors tourism service , ticket price discounting and seeking new marketers, rebranding is the creation od a new look and feel for an established airline tourism service from the airline's competitors.

The airline service life cycle extension strategies also may include these methods to help the airline organization to grow or grow up or develop its airline tourism market rapidly, e.g. repackaging and new sizes, the appearance of airline tourism service can be crucial gaining a passenger's attention and developing tourism interest , new formulas or additional airline tourism features to the tourism country, lower ticket prices to maintain interest or liquidate surplus stock new airline tourism service advertising campaign, altering the new airline channel of destination, such as online ticket purchase. Hence, after COVID 19 human disease had been skilled by new medicine , any airline organizations need to consider how to choose the most suitable strategy from different kinds of key strategies to expand their airline new tourism channels throughout the different airline tourism service life stages, in these four distinct stages: introduction, growth, maturity and decline or possible death stage, when this COVID 19 human disease had occurred from 2019 end, it may influence global travelers number had significant been reducing to bring any airline organizations may enter the decline life service cycle stage rapidly, even death life service cycle stage comes consequently.

Any airline organizations can use various marketing strategies in each stage to try to prolong the life cycle or attempt to reach the mature life cycle stage in short time. Avoiding to experience decline life service cycle stage, such as the COVID 19 human disease occurrence causes global travelers number began to reduce. It is ensure that any airline organizations do not expect to experience or reach the decline service life stage due to this COVID 19 human disease influences. The question is that how the airline organizations can maintain a strategy in the decline stage , such as COVID19 human disease influences global travelers number reduced and it brings many airlines income began to reduce, for example, reducing the airline promotional expenditure in this COVID 19 human disease occurrence period, reducing the number of airline distribution outlets , e.g. Hong Kong to New York airline flight channel reduces implementing ticket price cuts to get passengers to but the maintaining the airline tourism service and waiting for airline competitors to withdraw from the global airline tourism market.

Thus, following the initial growth, in this COVID human disease occurrence period, when the new airline organization enterprise enters the expansion stage during which the routing operation succeeds. The new airline organization can either reach the mature life service cycle stage either it can prolong to stay in this stage or it can not prolong to stay and enters to decline service life cycle stage , even death service life cycle stage. So , how to avoid the decline service life cycle stage comes to the new airline organization in this COVID 19 human disease occurrence period. It is any airline organizations concerning question when they are experiencing in the mature life cycle stage, but when COVID 19 human disease occurs to influence global travelers number began to reduce. May the airline organization experience the decline service life cycle stage rapidly when the COVID 19 human disease occurs ? It depends on whether it's strategies implementation are effective , its' strategies are effective, it may avoid to reach the decline life service cycle stage in short time easily due to COVID 19 human disease influences.

For this COVID 19 human mouth disease case , since 2019 had occurred, it brought serious tourism industry economic loss to any countries, many people loss jobs, many people feel fear to enter any shops when they are in crowd shop environment, e.g. restaurants can not permit to allow many people to sit closely, because when one person has COVID 19 human mouth disease, he can bring this disease to another person from air. So, many restaurants lose many clients in morning, lunch and night busy eating time, even ships also can not permit many people to enter their ships, because they avoid many people may contact, if one or some people has/have COVID 19 mouth disease, when he/she talks to the salespeople in the shop. It has high chance to cause many people get COVID human disease by mouth. So, any shops can not allow crowd in themselves shops to avoid any people have COVID 19 human disease occurrence. So, this COVID 19 human mouth disease may influence many businesses are experiencing decline life cycle stage, because clients number is continue decreasing, unless drug invention succeeds to fill this kind human mouth disease. Otherwise, on the consequence, many businesses will face death life cycle stage in short time possible. So, it is good example to explain unpredicted external environmental factor to bring global businesses will face decline life cycle in 2020 or next year, even after two years latter. So, COVID -19 human mouth disease may also influence any businesses had been experiencing long time in the mature life cycle to change to decline life cycle stage in possible. Instead of the businesses are experiencing in either birth or growth life cycle stage. for example, UK Cathay airline had been experiencing long time in the mature life cycle stage from 2000, when its clients number had been increasing, but when the end of 2019, COVID-19 human mouth and air contact disease had occurred in global to influence any people feel fear to catch airplanes to travel or business travel frequently, due to airplanes have none windows, its none window environment will bring COVID-19 disease to any passengers when the airplane has many passengers are sitting together closely, if anyone has COVID-19 disease, he will cause any one airplane service waiter, passenger , even pilot to have COVID-19 disease easily.

So, global airline industry is experiencing decline life cycle stage. even Cathay airline is one big UK developed airline , it's passengers number is large in the past, but when COVID-19 disease occurs to cause travelers number had been decreasing. Hence, Cathay airline is experiencing decline life cycle stage from mature life cycle stage. It needs to implement dismissing staffs to keep salaries expenditure reducing strategy in global, e.g. HK will have 4,000 front line airline service staffs or airport check in service staffs , they will be dismisses in HK Cathay airline market. Although, HK government had given money to support it to continue to alive in order to avoid dismissing employees decision . But, Cathay airline had made decision that it will dismiss many airline service staffs in different countries. In fact, if Cathay airline expects it would not reach to the decline life cycle stage later, this dismissing employees strategy aims to avoid spending much salaries expenditure , it may be one good method to avoid decline , even death life cycle stage occurs in this year or latter.

On conclusion, it is difficult to predict what factors may cause the business itself will face decline life cycle stage occurrence in any time. Hence, any businesses ought to spend time to research whether which methods or strategies can help them to continue to expand their market or fight any kinds of threats in those four identified business life cycle stages. To avoid business can not continue develop or die, when the business is experiencing in the decline life cycle stage, the strategy is that , the organization needs to spend time to observe or learn how and why its market environment is changing in order to make the most accurate or effective strategies decisions to solve any challenges in any one of these four life cycle stages successfully.

● How new economic development in oil industry

The future global economic growth, it will influence personal incomes and GDP rise. They would carry different weight in different countries at different times. Starting from low levels of incomer and economic development. Household consumption will change from being dominated by basic heat to rapidly rising energy use for higher levels of comfort in space heating and cooling (and large dwellings), and greater use of electrical appliances, finally to a degree of saturation influenced by the income distribution patterns of the country concerned. Income distribution typically changes very slowly, so that the technical market for heart will never be saturated because there will always be a proportion of poor people living in small spaces less comfortably than the average. Industrial energy consumption will be influenced by technical efficiency within each sector, and by changes in the structures of the economy, e.g. changing proportions of agriculture, heavy and light industry, and services. One may eventually see evidence of diminishing marginal returns to additional energy inputs compared to other inputs. Energy consumption in the energy transformation sector may be influenced by income, which drives the demand for electricity to influenced by income, which drives the demand for electricity to grow faster than the demand for heat, but is also subject to the chosen technology of transformation, which is influenced by the cost and availability of primary energy inputs (fuels) in new economic development environment.

IN new economic development environment, it will influences that fuels do not compete in all sectors; for example, the transport sector is dominated by oil. Nuclear and hydroelectric power (and most renewables) reach the user through electricity; electricity itself competes with the direct burning of fossil fuels. Electricity provides the means by which other fuels can compete with oil and gas in sectors, such as space heating and process heat. It also is the only means of powering applications such as motors, computers and lighting: these subsectors are difficult to analyze. However, there is strong evidence that higher incomes do not weaken the demand for electricity so much as the demand for energy in total (in contrast to the effect on the demand for non-electric energy forms).

Econometricians look at the historical record of change in fuel prices and quantities to distinguish several factors between the new economic development and old economic development to oil industry in the future. An income effect. Increasing (reducing) fuel prices reduces (increases) the purchasing power of consumers' income: higher incomes caused by lower prices will increase energy consumption; the consumers' allocation of the increased income to energy purchases may reduce as income rises. Thus income may be heading in a different direction from fuel prices that the effect of fuel price changes when incomes are rising means simply that rising incomes have increased demand. Reducing the cost of using energy through win-win efficiency measures causes a similar problem . On the consequence, in future new economic development environment, it may influence in both cases demand will be less than if the future oil price or efficiency has not changed. The other effect is that an efficiency or substitution effect. An increase in fuel prices may cause consumers to spend more on new equipment, building materials and management operations, which will reduce the amount of fuel required to give the same energy result to the user. The extent of the efficiency effect depends on what happens to the price of the new equipment or building: if those price s rise in line with the fuel price, changes in the balances between fuel and capital or management will not occur. A new user technology , such as the development of the combined cycle gas turbine generator may increase efficiency and thus greatly reduce the quantity of primary fuel needed to produce the required output in this case electricity. If electricity prices had remained sticky, and the electricity and gas markets were not competitive, some of this advantages could have accrued to the gas suppliers in the form of an increase in price, because th4 unit of gas produces more output of electricity, it would have a higher value. In reality, the development of new economic competitive environment in both gas and electricity has tended to ensure that the benefits of such technical advanced accrue to the consumer through lower final prices. The same many apply in the case of improved efficiency in future non-manual driving auto vehicle development: the consumer's cost of motoring is reduced in new economic non-manual driven auto vehicle (Artificial intelligent vehicle) can replace manual driven vehicle , even electricity battery can replace oil energy to be used in vehicles. So, oil price may be influenced to reduce in future new economic development environment.

New and old economic theories explain oil is not main factor to influence tourism income

● Can economic theory explain old price change to influence tourism income?

I shall attempt to apply old and new economic theory to explain whether oil changing price has direct relationship to influence global tourism indusry development or tourism income as below:

Is oil changing price the main to influence tourism income or tourism development or economic growth ? If oil price rises ar falls, it will or won't cause tourism income decreases or increases? If they have cause and effect relationship, what are the main factors to influence tourism income changes by oil price rises or falls ?

I aim to investigate how any why among oil price shocks will influence tourism income variables. We may distinguish between these oil price shocks: Supply-side , aggregate demand and oil specific demand shocks. I assume that oil specific demand shocks affect inflation and the tourism sector equity index. By constrast, I also believe that aggregate demand oil price shock exercisr an effect, either directly and indirectly tourism generated income and economic growth. So, in old economic theory, supply-side , aggregate demand view to oil specific demand shocks will influence tourism income varies. So, governments ought implement strategies against future oil price movements or plan for economic policy development.

In fact, instead of oil price changes will influence tourism income, it could also harm economic growth and tourism activities, due to the effect they expert on transporation, production cost, economic uncertainty.Because tourism activities is one important sector to influence any country's leisure consumption GDP income source. So, sudden fluctations in oil prices may also influence economic growth. It is based a hyphthesis known as the tourism led economic growth. So, it seems that they have direct or indirect relationship to case effect between oil price and tourism activities and development. So, increase on tourism income, the called " economic-driven tourism growth". In addition, high oil prices are affecting certain tourism industry segments , e.g. airlines, cruises lines, hotel, rent travelling car services etc. for oil, importing countries example, with reference to macro economic effects, higher oil prices generally lead to higher inflation, when they negatively influence to country's income.

Hence, from a micro-economic perspective, positive oil price shocks lead to a decline in disposable income. for low income people, it will bring an immediate and negative impact on tourism, mainly due to they feel tourism leisure is regarded as a luxury good, when oil price shocks to rise suddenly . It influences any airline or cruise entertainment service providers' costs are influenced to raise. Then, they need to increase air ticket or cruise ticket price. It will bring on negative tourism leisure demands-side the oil price increases low income group, potential tourism leisure consumers. Hence, it seems that oil price may have indirect relationship to influence tourism leisure consumers' needs.

In conclusion, the factors can influence travelers who decide to choose to travel the country, which include personal safety was perceived to the highest motivation factors among the important factors which include, scenic beauty, cultural interests, friendliness of local people, price of trip, services in hotels and restaurants, quality and variety of food and shopping facilities and services. The factors include both push and pull. Push factors include knowledge, prestige, and enhancement of human relationship etc., whereas, the most significant pull factors include high technologic image, expenditure and accessibility etc. For example, Japanese travelers visiting Hong Kong. Push factors are such as exploration dream fulfillment and pull factors are such as benefits sought, attractions and good climate city. It will be the factor of future travel patterns and motivations of sub-cultural and ethic groups for Japanese choice to go to Hong Kong travelling.

Bibliography

Backman, K., Backman, S., Uysal, M. And Sunshine, K. (1995). Event Tourism : An Examination Of Motivations And Activities. Festival Management And Event Tourism, 3(1), 15-24.

Fishbein, M., & Ajzen, Z. (1975). Belief, Attitude, Intention And Behaviour: An Introduction To Theory And Research, Boston: Addison Wesley.

Hsu, C.H.C., Cai , L.A., Li, M(2010). Expectation, Motivation And Attitude: A Tourist Behavioral Model. Journal Of Travel Research, 49(3), 282-296. http://dx.doi, org/10.1177/004728750 9349266.

ICT Information And Communication Technology Switzerland, 2005. ICT Fakten (ICT facts). Available from http://www.ictswitzerland.ch/de/ict%2fakten/factsfigures.asp(retrieved Dec.12, 2005) in German.

Lind, (2001): Befolkningen, Familjen, Livscykeln- Och Ekonomisk Tillvaxt. Institutet For Tillvaxtpo-litiska studier/Vinnova/Nutek.

Lohmann, Martin (2001): The 31 st. Reiseanalyse-RA 2001. Tourism: vol. 49, no.1/2001;pp.65-67, Zagreb.

United Nations Population Division (2001). World Population Prospects: The 2000 year Revision, New York.

Weber E.U., & W, P.Bottom (1989). "Axiomatic Measures Of Perceived Risk: Some Tests And extensions." journal of behavioral decision making, 2 (2): 113-31.

However, green or nature tourism strategy may include these elements : Quality, tourism should have an impact on the quality of life for all members of the tourist process, exploitation of nature resources should be optimal and ensure their generation, balance, distribution of benefits among participants in the tourist process must be fair. So, future any kinds of green or nature tourism will need have these features in order to attract many travelers to visit any countries' green lands, e.g. they may rent cars to travel to green lands. So, developing attractive green lands will be one kind new travelling trend for green tourism in global future travel market.

There are two types of models that contribute to the better understanding of future tourism industry development, explanatory model refer to factors that cause development growth. For example, whether the travelers feel necessary to travel to different destinations, very often nice landscapes and sightseeing, pescriptive modes (e.g. life clcle explanations, physical models) examines tourism from what appears on ground e.g. large hotels facilities etc. Hence, any kinds of tourism leisure must need build these both models in order to attract travelers to choose to buy the tourism package from the travel agent more easily. It is important tourism leisure element to any one travel agent's tourism service package if it hopes to develop its tourism service success. So, the expansion of the tourist region over the natural boundaries of the city centre that occured in the first place as a result of the growth of tourism demand, is the end causing this very expansion to continue. Butler (1980) involves a six stage evoluation of tourism, namely explanation, involvement, development, consolidation, stagnation, and post-stagnation. The last stage is further characterized by a period of decline, rejuvenation or stabilization. The applicability of the model to a given area has been assessed and judged of a tourist destination's development matched the six phases conceptually described by Butler

reference

Butler, R.W. (1980). the concept of a tourist area cycle of evolution: Implications for management of resources. Canadian Geographer, 24, 5-12.

Hence, our tourism industry is facing decline life cycle stage because COVD 19 human mouth disease has influenced many travelers feel fear to catch airplanes to travel, even they also feel to contact the potential COVD 19 human mouth disease people when they arrive the country , they feel that they may contact these sick people, instead of airplanes. So, this kind disease had influenced many travel agents reduce tourism service package number , due to many travelers' tourism leisure activities will reduce, due to travelers number reduces, they only carry cargos to transport to replace travelers COVD 19 disease influence our tourism industry is experiencing decline life cycle stage nowadays. Unless, COVD 19 human mouth attacking to lung disease can be treated by new medicine invention . Otherwise, tourism industry can not re-grow to mature life cycle stage easily.

The most used framework for examing stagnation and possible decline in tourism destinations has been tourist area life cycle model (Butler, 1980). The model has been operationalized frequently in the tourism lierature. It includes series of stages in tourism development, leadning eventually to the stagnation and post-stagnation stages. When a nature destination can either decline, however, it does not offer a systematic explanation of hoe tourism destination might avoid decline . Such as COVD 19 human mouth disease may influence travelers feel fear to catch air planes. So, even the country has beautiful nature scene to attract people to travel, althoug it is a nature attractive destination, but due to COVD19 disease occurs, it may influence this country's this nature attractive destination to enter decline life cycle stage at this moment.

Hence, tourism industry's life cycle stage , sometime it can be influenced by non predicted factor, such as COVD19 disease factor, it can influence travelers' travelling desire to be reduced suddenly from 2019 , due to they feel afraid to catch air planes to avoid to get this kind COVD 19 human mouth disease to bring lung disease when they are sitting in closed window inside air plane environment. So, COVD 19 human counth disease causes global tourism industry is facing serious decline life cycle stage. The question is that any one does not know when this kind COVD 19 disease will be treated by new medicine invention, so if this kind COVD 19 disease still can not be killed by new medicine invention, then it will continue to influence global tourism development to be improved , even any nature attractive scenes, they can not persuade any travelers to catch air planes to visit any countries to travel easily. But, however, we still need to keep our natural environment to prepare future COVD 19 diease disappears , e.g. parks are important places for the protection of ecological systems and natural resources as well as for the provision ot recreational and tourism opportunities for the public. Then, nature or green tourism can be continue to develop to attract many travelers to travel after COVD 19 disease disappears in the future.

● What are the characteristics of birth life cycle stage to tourism industry ?

Butler , R.W. (1980)'s model begins with a discovery and exploration or birth stage in which a location is discovered by a small, select group of people as a place with desirable assets often, this discovery is nature population who may see the perceived assets. As just ordinary aspects of their environment or local culture. The early tourists have very little support in the form of amenities, and typically, this is preferred and is part of a location's of being undiscovered. The early tourists, therefore rely heavily on and interact frequently with the residents of the region. This small group of early tourists is largely in dependent and shares information about a destination by word of mouth or by select affinity groups. Over time, as more people are introduced to the destination, the number of visitors begins to increase. So " word of mouth" will be traveler information to persuade them to make travelling destination choices in the tourism industry beginning. It is tourism industry's birth life cycle stage characteristics . However, internet invention can let any one see any countries' scene photos, so it is one kind of good advertisement method to introduce any countries' scene, instead of travelling magazine in tourism growth and maturity life cucle both stages.

Moreover, space tourism is at the birth life cycle stage. It needs travelers feel interest to travel space, if this kind space tourism service providers hope to implement their any space journeys in success. These factors may influence its development succeeds. Nowadays, its target market is wealthy travelers group, wealthy individual are needed, as they serve as the main consumers for space tourism . For space tourism to succeed there must be enough demand from those who are able to afford to expensive ticket. To date there have only been seven commercial space travelers, or space tourists, although they prefer to be called space flight participant, as they see themselves as pioneers and adventers as opposed to ordinary tourists. So, any future space tourism that price must need to reduce to general public, e.g. ordinary income level people, they can spend, if space tourism hopes to reach from stage stage rapidly. So, space tourism is still far to mature stage.It depends on whether how long time its any space journey ticket price can be reduced to any one can pay. So, when its customer target is not only wealthy travelers, many ordinary or common income level people, they can pay to any one space jounrney. It may mean to reach growth life cycle stage.

● What characteristics to space tourism growth stage?

When human space tourism of commericalization of activities in outer space can bring these feeling to let any one space traveler feels then, it may mean that it can reach growth stage, such as they may feel their any space journeys may bring positive impacts that outer. Space recreation can produce, in order to come up with space tourism, exploring and untravelling the hidden anystories of the space are needed. Also they can feel need drastically broadens and enrichs human's technical awareness and constructive knowledge need from any one space tourism journey package.

When space tourism reachs mature life cycle stage? What its characteristics are? When any one space travelers can feel that not only earth based attractions that simulate the space experience , they must need to catch airships to experience this different tourism experience, such as space theme parks, space training camps, virtual reality facilities , space hotels (skotel), multimedia interactive games and tele robotic moon rovers controlled from earth, but also parabolic flights, lasting up to three days or week long stay at floating space hotel, including participatory educational ,as well as sports competitions (i.e. space olympics). Hence, above these will be nay space tourism development. It can reach mature life cycle stage characteristics when any one can feel the real travelling mouth to compare to travel our earth anywhere, they can not find that they feel space tourism may be same to our earth's holiday (need to rela) or cultural (know different places or specialized tourism, e.g. expectations of adventures , even space scientists discover new experiences to expectations of adventure or get more information, scientific interest feeling. Then, at this moment, we can call space tourism has reached the mature stage. However, I believe that to develop space tourism in success. We must need to control space tourism ticket price to be reduced to general low income people. They may spend budget level. So, ticket price may be one major factor to influence future space tourism growth when it can reach mature stage. Also, it mean that whether space tourism may become another kind of popular tourism lesiure activities to use. It depends on ticket price factor, instead of its any space tourism trip arrangement factor. So, any one space tourism service provider must need long time to spend in order to implement its different strategies, e.g. ticket price, space trip arrangemet to achieve its their space tourism to achieve its their space tourism different destination package in success if they hope their future space tourism business can grow up in short time.

CHAPTER SIX

Airport service influences traveler destination choice

Airport service life cycle stage improvement strategy

Any organizations will have life cycle stage from birth, growth , mature to decline. In airport service organizations have theis life cycle stages in service aspect. Airports organizatins aim to provide safe, comfortable , even shopping environment to let passengers to stay and to wait to transfer another air planes to visit another destination or arrive the country's airport to check out or check in to enter the airport to leave. If airports have life cycle stages, what the characteristics to every stage? How to improve airport service in order to reach mature life cycle stage rapidly? How to implement airport service strategy in order to reach mature life cycle stage to the aorport organization rapidly?I shall explain as below:

Any airports need to be planned in order to raise excellent service to let passengers to let any travelers choose to travel the country whether the country can provide excellent service and facilities. It will bring indirect emotion impact to influence the travelers chooce to revisit the country to travel again. However, soft or hard element or) staff service performance or airport facility), they will influence whether the different countries travelers to choose to travel to re-visit the country again. So, learning how to keep the mature or airport service life cycle stage to stay long time, it will be one important factor to influence any airport business in success.

In the birth life style stage to airport, airport organizations must maintain the capability to provide expert advice to airport owners an matters including operational safety, during construction, environmental compatibility, and airport development standards. No other private or public organization can be expected maintain this level of proficiency. These value-added services enhance public trust when assuring consistant application of standards for the nation's airport system. So, it seems that when the new airport is built if it hopes its passenger customers can consider themselves emotion need. So, it ought concentrate on nowadays airplane landing cunways or airport transfer free service transport etc. facilities can let them to feel safe when they were walking in any airport places. If they feel anywhere are dangerous when they are walking or staying in the ne sirport, then new airport non safe or dangerous factor may influence travelers to choose the country to travel again.

Any new airports will need have good new national airport plan in order to it might operate in the near future with respect to safety areas. The plan elements may include as below:

Achieving zero accidents aim, establish standard safety areas at all commercial service airports , achieving the most minimum 85% of all passenger flights operate on runways with safe feeling, increase measure to 100% of all passenger flight operating on runways with standard safety areas after three months. Within 5 years, 95% of all passenger flights begin and end on runways with standard safety areas.

On benefits aspect, aims to mobilize work force to improve safety area performance describes realistic investment benefits. So, in any new airports birth life cycle stage, they must need to consider safety and expenditure for repair aspect in order to keep its service performance to avoid passengers have dissatisfactory feeling when they are staying in their new airports.

When the country has many travelers travel to the country , then the country's new airport passengers number must increase. It is its the new airport growth life cycle stage. These are critical success factors influence the airport, whether it can improve service performance in order to excite different countries travelers visiting the country's airport desire or grow up the visitors number successfully. The critical success factors may include: Having necessary support from internal and externa stakeholders to implement and willing to share information and identify anywhere the total airport facilities of repair needs that are both reliable and feasible projections to let passengers to feel more safe feeling when they are staying in the airport, understand its future service vision and mission, set strategic direction and goals to process/ product specific objectives and decision-making across and doen the organization, define, model and prioritize planning prcesses critical for mission performance, practice hand-on sernior management ownership of planning process and allow field, personnel flexiblity in performing jobs, adjust organizational structures , an essessment program to evaluate planning process and product management , e.g. national airport system performance, create organizational understanding of the value management to customer and stakeholder current and future expectations developing human resources management strategies to support new process that solves needs planners and engineers, building information resources strategies change, especially for entering data at the source and maintains data integrity and timeliness.,establish central support group to support reengineering efforts, outreach and training efforts across the organization, phase in short-and long-term results that achieve set goals and objectives over the next two years.

Thus, when one new airport begins to feel passengers number is increasing. It ought experience the growth life cycle stage to the new airport , if it hopes that it can reach mature life cycle stage rapidly as well as keeps its mature life cycle stage to stay in this stage long time or reachs the airport service performance to the most satisfactory level in this mature life cycle stage. It must need to attempt to plan these strategies to implement in order to avoid decline life cycle stage occurs in short time. So, it explains why some new airport can experience the development to mature life cycle stage from grow life cycle stage in short time,even when it reachs mature life cycle stage. It can keep to stay in this stage long time. The reason is that it had prepared effective strategies to achieve how to improve its airport service performance aim in order to satisfy passenger needs. When they are staying in the country's airport any time. Hence, every year revising service performance is needed to any airports.

Any airports must have development processes. The question is that whether the airport needs how long time to reach growth or mature life cycle stage from birth stage or decline life cycle stage will be delayed how long to occur. The development processes may mean that the airport development life cycle stages changes that had toard a particular result or even as a series of continuous actions or operations coducting to an end (Merriam-Webster, 2013).

reference

Merriam-webster (2013). On line dictionary. Available at: https://www.merriam-webster. com/(last accessed July , 8 2013).

Hence, any airport organizations with experience development pricess. When the new airport is built, it must be in the birth life cycle stage. Its passengers number can not increase rapidly. It needs time to grow their number. But, when the new airport operates a period, many different countries begin feel this new airport is existence in the country. They will attempt to catch airplance to visit this country airport to catch airplane to visit tis country airport to travel. If they feel this country airport service performance can satisfy their short time staying feeling or its passengers or airports visitors number may increase rapidly. It meand that this airport is experiencing growth life cycle stage. So, if the airport can attract many visitors in short time. It will reduce time to growth life cycle stage from birth life cycke stage.

So , service performance may be one important factor to inflow the airport grows. When the airport develops to the period, passengers number can not increase rapidly, it may be the airport's mature life cycle stage. Due to it's passengers number can not grow rapidly, its passengers number also may reduce. When its passengers number has significant decrease, if its reduction number is increasing more. It implies that the airport is experiencing decline life cycle stage. All any country's airport may experience whole life cycle stages. If the country's airport can not implement successful strategies, it may experience birht life cycle stage in long time because it can not grow its passengers number significantly. So, any airports need to learn how to help them to change growth life cycle stage, even mature life cycle stage can stay in long time easily. If they hope to attract many different countries passengers to visit their airports or travel themselves countries or enjoy to stay short time in themselves airports in order to grow themselves airline industry development.

● How can processes improvement management strategy influence airport service performance?

Overall processes in an airport may involve passengers, luggage, cargo, aircraft movements, ground handling, and crews . All of these operations can be systematised into processes at airport terminal. Three main types of processes can be established departing , arrival and transfer . Departure consists in catching a flight to a final or intermediate destination, arrival consists in landing and leaving the airport, and transfer consists in landing at the airport only to catch another flight to a final or an intermediate destination. Airports also deal with cargo. It involves in the movement of cargo by air, cargo fies from the shopper to the consignee through one or more airlines. However, when the airport can let them freight forwarder, being familiar with the necessary procedures how permits the airline to concentrate on the provision of air transport and to avoid time consuming details of the facilitation and landside distribution system. It will raise efficiency and improve service performance. The services product by the ground handling are crucial to the success and efficiency of the airport operations.

These services are usually provided by specialised companies. Briefly, it includes the luggage treatment, passengers carrying from plan to terminal when needed and aircraft assistance. Also, focusing on crew, there are two majoe processes, one for departures and the other for arrivals. The crew members also have to pass the security and passport controls. However, they have special channels for this. Once they reach the aircraft, the similarities with the passengers' procedure stop. Hence, they have to perform a set of activities , such as check the aircraft load sheets and help passengers to name a few. Also airport terminal operations processes for passengers and luggage, typically for departures , passengers do the check on the airline area, pass security controls, proceed to the general lounge and lastly to the gate holding area. arriving passengers are able to immediately go from the luggage claim area, but the non-passengers have to pass the passport control at first. After this passengers have to decide if they need to declare goods or not as the paths are different . Hence, if the airport can reduce all of this service processes are less complex as immigration check in-out service, liggage claim can be efficient to carry when passengers need to find themselves luggage. Then, it will reduce waste time and let they satisfy airport service absolutely. So, reducing service process time amy also help the airport to increase customers number significantly. When airport role is the middleman between airlines , cargo transport service providers and passengers, e.g. short time transport cargo service and reducing passengers check in or check out service time. then, it will let them to feel more satisfactory service to the airport.

Hence, airport capacity is as a multifactor function leaves open the exact relationship between the factors but stresses that all factors are relevant to assess airport capacity . So , understanding airport capacity and what drives the capacity usage at airports may provide an insight in the set of instructments available to optimise the use of capacity. All of these factors may influence any capacity of an airport, they may include as below:

For example, technical constraints, e.g. ATM per hour service in a runway in a combined arrival and departure fashion, when many passengers are staying at the airport, they can withdraw money from ATM easily. So, ATM number facilities service supply number and location choice to the airport factors will infuence passengers ' satisfactory level, another factor is environmental constraints, it can directly offer the wellbeing of the communities surrounding the negative emotion to passengers and communities surrounding the airprt. For this factor, the change in technology and/or operational procedures can provide more capacity in the system.

Airline business models factor, it can affect the capacity spoke model when other under a point-point one ,these models directly affect the peak hour operational capacity, particularly in big international hubs. Airlines often compete with high frequencies between destinations, thus increasing the number of movements. In addition, conncectivity also has downsides for this model: the delays in one airport might be exported and sometimes in another, due to the connectivity influencing the real capacity. This factor has been setting economic incentives or pricing models. Furthermore, expanding information systems, from one airport to multiple airports gate-to-gate concept, and the use of larger airport to redcuce frequencies.

Hence, above these factors may influence whether the airport needs how long time to reach maturiry life cycle stage when it is staying the growth life cycle stage. It depends on how its strategies implementation and how environment influence its implementation , if it hopes to achieve to reach the maturity life cycle stage in success in short time.

Finally, I shall explain life cycle cst analysis to any country pavement strategy will bring what significant influential benefits to any airports continue to develop in order to avoid to reach decline life cycle stage time in short time easily , when they are staying in the mature life cycle stage. In the construction or rehabilitation investments of highway's pavements, it is already common to perform a life-cycle analysis or life cycle cost analysis for different alternatives to airport pavements. Becauae when any airport pavements are using for a long time, every day has many airplanes need to fly to land on the pavement. It can bring significant repace influence when the airport has many airplanes are needed to land on the pavements every day in the maturity life cycle stages.

Hence, how to evaluate the repair cost expenditure budget in order to satisfy every day air planes land on the airport pavement need. In the calculations are different cost factors (including direct and indirect cost)to any airport itself pavement. Direct costs are related to the critical construction cost landing on pavement activities and are calculated with information from the airport agency and constructors that work for them. The indirect costs are related with the loss of daily revenue of the airport during work activities, such as landing on the airport pavement.

Runways are the most critical pavements area of airport , so it is critical to ensure the quality of these pavement to let airplanes to land on the airport safety, e.g. they need to be constructed with sufficient strength to carry the moving airport and have a high resistance to skidding and aquaplaining. It is most of the time accomplished with reconstructions or deep rehabilitation. Hence, predicting how much will spend on airport pavement facilities expenditure must need in every day.

However, the life cycle assessment (LCA) is a mult step procedure for calculating the life time environmental impact of a product or service is needed to any airport organizations, when they reachs maturity life cycelt stage . The complex process includes goal and cope definition in inventory analysis impact assessment. The process is vaturally iteractive as quality and completeness of information is constantly being testes. When the definition of the aim and scope of the study is done the next step is the development of an inventory, in which all significant environmental burdens during the lifetime of the product,, such as airport pavements or process , such as airplanes landing on the pavement or airplanes leaving from the pavement in the airport.

(Araujo, Oliveria & Silve) 2014 explained that life cycle snslysis of pavements are focused on the activities of extraction, production, transportation application of materials, concisely the construction of the road. Because its difficult to obtain other relevant data knowing that the use phase of the pavement is predominant with repect to energy consumption and also to gas emissions related to the atmosphere. One of the main factors for the use phase is the rolling resistance, this depends on the surface and structural characteristics of the different pavements.

Hence, , if the airport can have good repairment or renew skills to help its pavement to improve. Then, it may bring long time benefit, such as reducing airplanes energy consumption and also to avoid gas emissions or reduce gas emissions accident occurrene, even air plane landing on pavement accident occurrence chance can reduce to the zero. so, defining the expected pavement performance time improvement strategy can influence whether the airport pavement can satisfy all airplane users how long time landing on or leaving on the airport pavement. Also it is the major factor to influence airport main function success for any airplanes arriving to the country's airport pavement or leaving from the country's airport pavement. Hence, calculating any airport pavement life cycle costs factor. It is necessary to analysis and interpret carefully the results to identfy the most economic pavement strategy in any airport's whole life cycle development stages.

reference

Araujo, J.P.C. Oliveria, J.R.M. & Silva H.M.R.D. (2011) . the importance of the use phase on the LCA of environmentally friendly solutions for asphalt road pavements. transportation research part D: trasport and environment, 32(0), 97-110. Retrieved in March 2015 from://

dx. doi.org/10.1016/j.trd.2014.07.006.